BOXING
THE LORD IN
AND OTHER WAYS WE HINDER

Revelation

STEPHEN K. HUNSAKER
With MICHELLE K. HUNSAKER

Boxing the Lord In: and Other Ways We Hinder Revelation
Stephen K. Hunsaker with Michelle K. Hunsaker

For permissions contact: verticallyconnected@gmail.com
Published by Vertically Connected Publishing
www.verticallyconnected.com
Printed by Book Printers of Utah
Cover Design by Evan McCain
Cover Photo licensed from Adobe Stock;
   taken by Eduardo Estellez in Turegano, Spain
ISBN 978-1-7324450-0-0 (paperback)
ISBN 978-1-7324450-1-7 (eBook)

ACKNOWLEDGEMENTS

This book is the collaborative effort of many people and their insights. I would like to personally thank:

First, and foremost, my wife, Michelle, my "Emma" — for her long-suffering and patience putting into one manuscript hundreds of random ideas and lessons I have developed and taught over the years. To say that this book would not exist were it not for her would be an understatement.

My children, for teaching me about what really matters in life and for their patience, encouragement, and willingness through this long process to allow their mother and I to go on hundreds of "dates" to "work on the book."

My parents, my mother, especially, who has always been (sometimes quite literally) my cheerleader, encouraging me, without any doubt in my ability, to reach the high expectations she has always had of me.

My good friend and colleague, Edward Hegemann, for his unfailing encouragement, Eric Richards, for his invaluable help pulling this work together in the final stages, friends and family who read and re-read portions of this book, and Danni Trainor-Buttars at ThinkWorthy Writing and Editing for the incredible insight, clarity, and purposeful direction she gave this book.

The thousands of students of all ages I have been blessed to teach over the years, who have, in turn, taught me from their stories, experiences, questions, and faith, and some of whom have been willing to share their voices in this book.

A small group of women who used to meet in the Relief Society room of the Garrisonville, Virginia church building for an adult Institute class every Wednesday morning. You will never know how much you influenced my journey of wanting to understand revelation better.

My God, for allowing me the privilege to be an instrument for good in His hands and for revealing to me the many ways I have hindered revelation in my own life while being eternally patient with me as He has tried to teach me.

DEDICATION

To our ten children
Stephen, Chelsea, Kaylee, TJ, Kenzie, Lindsay,
Joshua, Joseph, Annalise, and Elisabeth —
our "hobbies," our "big-red-van-full," our whole world —
that they may know to what source they need to look in this life.
For we, like Nephi, labor diligently to write so that we might
persuade our children to believe in, trust, and know
their Father, the only true God,
and their Savior, Jesus Christ, whom He has sent.

TABLE OF CONTENTS

PREFACE

I am, and always will be, a teacher. My favorite place to be, besides with my family, is in the classroom. In fact, I feel a little like Moroni: much more confident in my ability to convey thoughts and ideas through the spoken word than through my awkward attempts at the written word (see Moroni 1:4).

Why, then, would I write a book? Because I have a deep desire to share some things I've learned from over 30 years of experiences teaching the gospel every day, raising ten incredible but very different children, obtaining degrees that study human behavior, and serving in various capacities in the Church all over the country. I've learned a lot about people, why we do what we do, and how to apply the gospel in everyday life. I've also learned, among other things, that many of us are working very diligently to receive revelation, yet many of us struggle with the process in some way.

Obviously from the title of this book, my purpose is to share ways we might hinder that revelation in our lives without meaning to. In no way am I an expert on the subject of revelation or even on ways we may hinder it. I often still struggle with it, don't always understand what the Lord is trying to tell me, and wonder why I am not getting answers from the heavens. (In fact, the process of writing this book was a continuous divine tutorial on asking for and receiving answers from the heavens over and over again.) There are also many aspects of revelation that we won't necessarily touch on here; this work isn't meant to be comprehensive by any means.

However, I have gained some insight throughout my life that I believe can make a difference for any of us as we strive to be more divinely guided in this life. I've seen firsthand how the concepts shared in this book have helped many people of all different ages and backgrounds understand why revelation might not be working in their lives — and in ways that often seem to have nothing to do with revelation. Indeed, these insights have completely changed *my* experience with personal revelation, and thus my relationship with my God. I am hoping they can do the same for you.

INTRODUCTION

"Pouring Down Knowledge from Heaven"

In the Doctrine and Covenants, the Lord declared, "No power can stay the heavens. . . . As well might man stretch forth his puny arm to stop the Missouri river in its decreed course, or to turn it up stream, as to hinder the Almighty from pouring down knowledge from heaven upon the heads of the Latter-day Saints" (D&C 121:33).

If you stop and really think about it, that heavenly visual is truly breathtaking. God is literally pouring down His divine wisdom and guidance from the heavens. He is communicating His purposes and desires. He is revealing His mind and will. Indeed, President Russell M. Nelson recently testified that of all the things he has felt since his new calling as President of the Church, the Spirit has repeatedly impressed upon his mind "how *willing* the Lord is to reveal His mind and will."[1]

This willingness really shouldn't come as any surprise to us. We worship a God whose most important eternal work is not the creation and progression of mountains, nations, or even universes (Moses 1:39). No, of all His creations, Elder Jeffrey R. Holland explained, "*we* are his prized possessions. . . . And of all the titles He has chosen for Himself, *Father* is the one He favors most."[2]

Indeed, His most important endeavor in all of eternity is the eternal progression of each one of us individually. He desires for us to become like Him so that we can inherit all that He has, including His eternal happiness, and enjoy the life that He lives.[3]

Because of both this divine love and our divine potential, God did not send us here into a tempting and dangerous world without a way to navigate through it back to Him.[4] It's simply not in His nature to leave us stranded.

Of the many gifts He has provided for us to help us on this journey, one of the most remarkable is the gift of the Holy Ghost. This third member of the Godhead has the sacred responsibility to be the *minister* and *messenger* of the Father and the Son.[5] Thus, through His Spirit, we can receive a "constant flow of daily guidance, caution, encouragement, strength, spiritual cleansing, comfort, and peace."[6] This guidance, this encouragement, this comfort, indeed this *revelation*, as Elder Neil L. Andersen testified, "is scattered among us."[7]

However, despite how willingly this divine communication is offered or how abundant it may be all around us, I have found even the most faithful and diligent among us sometimes struggle receiving, understanding, and acting on it. Indeed, revelation doesn't always seem to be flowing in our lives the way it is flowing down from the heavens.

How could it be that something so willingly offered is not always easy to find or receive?

As I have wrestled with this question over the years — trying to gain a better understanding of how personal revelation works and even more importantly why it doesn't — I've come to at least one conclusion. We may not be able to hinder the Almighty from pouring down revelation from the heavens, however, it is entirely possible to hinder that revelation *in our own lives*, much like shutting a door or covering a window blocks out the sunlight in a room.

Sometimes the things we do — whether intentional or not — may not have the power to stop the glorious sun from shining, but they can prevent much of its warmth and illumination from coming into our lives.

DEVELOPING THIS MOST IMPORTANT SKILL

When you think about it, even though one of our Father's greatest priorities is to communicate with His children, receiving and understanding the mind and will of an eternal Being is not necessarily going to be easy for us mere mortals. His thoughts are not our thoughts; neither are His ways our ways. They are often higher and holier than we can fully comprehend, especially on our own.[8]

When He reveals His purposes to us, God is literally sharing portions of His insight and His perspective with us from where He stands seeing all of eternity. When He guides us, it seems He is helping us know what He would feel, say, or do if He were in our situation. When He teaches us, He is often teaching us about the very inner workings of His divine character — knowledge that can lead to a change in our very natures.[9] Revelation is at least one way God is teaching us about Himself.

Having access to that kind of divine information is a wonderful blessing! Understanding that kind of divine information is a wonderful challenge! Elder Gerald N. Lund even taught that one of the greatest challenges of learning how to come unto Christ and be perfected in Him is to learn how to hear, recognize, and then follow His voice.[10]

It seems, in fact, to be a *skill* that must be developed, much like the skill President James E. Faust developed as a young boy to tune a crystal radio set. He explained that in order to pick up a radio station, he had to scratch a tiny receiving wire whisker over the top of a small bumpy crystal to find the right pinpoint. Often, this precise spot was a low or high point on the crystal. If he was just one millimeter off on either side of that point, he would lose the signal and only hear static.

However, "over time, with patience and perseverance, good eyesight, and a steady hand, [he] learned to find the signal point on the crystal" and was able to hear the station; "so it is," President Faust said, "with divine communication."[11]

We have to learn how the process of revelation works. We must learn to recognize not only what the Lord's voice sounds like, but also when and where and how He speaks to *us*. Sister Julie B. Beck even taught, "The ability to qualify for, receive, and act on personal revelation is the single most important skill that can be acquired in this life."[12]

We must also at some point begin to recognize what we are doing and not doing that might be hindering that process. Learning these skills and making these discoveries requires investing some of the same patience, concentration, time, and willingness to learn from trial-and-error that President Faust invested learning how to receive a radio signal.

No wonder, then, that we might struggle with revelation from time to time. In this process of learning, sometimes we are going to misunderstand; sometimes, we are going to get it wrong or do it wrong. Receiving revelation is not necessarily complicated; if anything, *we* make it complicated. Yet, it is not something that will come without some practice. It is work — spiritual work — if ever there was any.[13]

Yes, we can also hinder revelation because of unworthiness.[14] Certainly, the ability to receive this kind of divine guidance requires us to meet some divine qualifications.[15] I don't think we have to be perfect or sinless to receive revelation, but it seems we won't be able to understand the higher, holier thoughts of God without rising in some way to meet those thoughts. (Indeed, being worthy to receive revelation does not seem to be about never being stained by sin, but rather about what efforts we make to continually cleanse ourselves from that sin.)

When we are not making some sincere effort to purify our lives, it will simply be more difficult to receive heaven's guidance clearly. However, as important and fundamental as that truth is in our experience with revelation, that kind of hindering is not our focus here.

RECOGNIZING OTHER KINDS OF HINDRANCES

We are going to concentrate, instead, on ways we hinder revelation without even realizing it. Although personal revelation can certainly be hindered because of lack of effort or sin, I believe it can also be hindered because of other things we are doing, believing, relying on, or worrying about that are actually obstructing that inspiration. Indeed, we can unknowingly get in the way of the very revelation we seek. These are the kinds of hindrances we are going to talk about in this book.

Some of these hindrances may not seem relevant to revelation at all, yet they interfere with it nonetheless, preventing divine communication from reaching us, making sense to us, or sometimes even mattering to us.

They are things like this:

- We block the very revelation we have been seeking for months by "boxing the Lord in."
- Our *"recipes"* unknowingly push God out of the picture or create unrealistic expectations of how He should guide or bless us.
- We aren't getting answers from heaven because we are actually looking everywhere *but* heaven for them.
- We unknowingly filter pure inspiration through false, unrealistic, or unhealthy ideas, distorting their meaning and causing confusion.
- We narrow the answers God can give us by wanting specifics.
- We miss out on personalized instruction because we make others' revelation *our* revelation.
- There isn't room for revelation in our minds because they are "encumbered."
- We get off track or prevent further divine guidance because we have given our own "reason" for a revelation.
- We miss the communication God is sending us because we are not "staying present."

After learning about some of these hindrances to revelation in a class, one man shared, "What I used to think was God's doing — like not getting any answers, feeling like He wasn't paying attention to my life, or being confused by a certain impression — has often been *my own doing*. And I didn't even realize it. This knowledge has improved my relationship with Him so much simply because I stopped blaming Him for not caring about me. It has helped me come to know God and trust Him better."

SURVIVING SPIRITUALLY IN COMING DAYS

Many years ago, President Boyd K. Packer, while acting as President of the Quorum of Twelve Apostles, prophetically declared,

"No one of us can survive in the world of today, much less in what it will soon become, without personal inspiration."[16]

More recently, President Russell M. Nelson re-emphasized this message when he testified: "If we are to have any hope of sifting through the myriad of voices and the philosophies of men that attack truth, we must learn to receive revelation. Our Savior and Redeemer, Jesus Christ, will perform some of His mightiest works between now and when He comes again. We will see miraculous indications that God the Father and His Son, Jesus Christ, preside over this Church in majesty and glory. But in coming days, *it will not be possible to survive spiritually without the guiding, directing, comforting, and constant influence of the Holy Ghost.*"[17]

You and I may only be starting to understand just how prophetic this counsel really is, but the adversary has already figured this out. He already knows what revelation actually is. He knows where it ultimately will lead God's children. And he does not want us to receive it! Thus, he will do whatever it takes to ruin our experience with it.

Surely, he will tempt us to sin so that we move ourselves away from divine instruction or feel unworthy to ask for it. Surely, he will distract us with worldly static. If he can, he will take advantage of our inexperience or lure us into complacency or mind-numbing activity. But he will also every day, and in every way, interfere with revelation much like a commander mounting a military invasion is intent on jamming the channels of communication of those he intends to conquer.[18]

It seems the adversary, if he cannot get us to disqualify ourselves from heavenly guidance, will distract us, deceive us, or distort the divine messages we so desperately need. In fact, could this be why our world is noisier, busier, crazier, and more superficially connected than at any other time in history? We cannot afford to be on the front lines in this "war" without communication from "headquarters." We cannot, in these last important battles, afford to give the adversary any power.

Yet, sometimes we do. We give him power when we lack understanding of this divine process. We do this when we haven't paid the price to know God or how He communicates with us. We give Satan this power when we don't know what could be interfering with the messages God is trying to send us.

So, some of the most important questions we can ask ourselves about this most important skill is: Do I recognize how, where, and when God speaks to His children? Do I correctly understand my role in relation to God's role? Do I know what to expect? And do I understand the doctrines associated with revelation? Being able to begin to answer these questions can bless us so much in this experience.

Fortunately, God is also giving us so many opportunities to learn how revelation works and develop this skill. He is providing us so many chances to use it! Think about the changes that have recently been made in the Church: missionaries are finding those looking for the truth *by revelation*, then teaching those that they find *by revelation*. Teachers are preparing lessons, asking questions, and facilitating discussions *by revelation*. Young Women's leaders are being asked to run girl's camp *by revelation*. The Lord is asking us to minister to each other *by revelation*. The list goes on and on.

From the looks of it, God is developing us into a people who, like Helaman's sons Nephi and Lehi, *live* by revelation, even that we are "having many revelations daily" (Helaman 11:23). Indeed, it seems we are meant to be connecting with the heavens on a constant basis, even "hour by hour" and "moment by moment," if necessary.[19] This must be one way we are going to, as the Prophet Joseph Smith taught, grow into this principle of revelation.[20]

Thus, we must do whatever it takes to understand it, use it, and become better at it. We must figure out how the Lord is speaking to us. And we must figure out what might be getting in the way of that revelation — whatever it may be. Elder Patrick Kearon even recently taught, "If there is something you carry in your heart that is blocking you — in any degree — from truly connecting with your Heavenly Father and feeling His love and His plan for you, resolve now to make it right."[21]

Let's resolve now to begin to make right anything that is not working in regards to revelation in our lives. Let's fine-tune ourselves better to that precious point of reception where we can hear His voice.

Let's discover and remove what might be covering up or blocking heaven's light. Let's make inspiration work better in our lives not only so that our lives can be better but also so that *we* can become better, even more like Him.

Therefore, What?

At the end of each chapter in this book, I will present additional insights about revelation that compel us to explore more deeply the doctrines and principles associated with revelation. I will also connect truths about revelation with other truths of the gospel. You will find questions to answer, thoughts to ponder, and almost always "homework" to do to deepen your understanding and make relevant, personal connections with the truths discussed.

This section is inspired in a way by a concept Elder Jeffrey R. Holland introduced in a C.E.S. Conference on the New Testament in 2000. After presenting a masterful discourse — as he always seems to do — on patterning our teaching after the Savior's example, he then shared this: "President Boyd K. Packer . . . has a question he often asks when we have made a presentation or given some sort of exhortation to one another in the Twelve. He looks up as if to say, 'Are you through?' And then he says to the speaker (and, by implication, to the rest of the group), 'Therefore, what?'

"'Therefore, what?' I think that is what the Savior answered day in and day out as an inseparable element of His teaching and preaching. . . . . These sermons and exhortations were to no avail if the actual lives of His disciples did not change."[22]

The concepts shared in this book will, in large measure, be to no avail if our lives do not change in some way. Thus, these additional ideas at the end of each chapter will challenge you to examine your perspective and think in ways you possibly haven't before. They will ask you to consider things you might unknowingly be thinking, believing, or doing that are hindering revelation in your life. They will require some work on your part. In my opinion, these insights and applications can be just as meaningful as the contents of the chapter itself.

Put yourself in the place where revelation flows. As I alluded to earlier in this introduction, there are actually many ways we can hinder revelation in our lives. We are going to talk specifically about a few less obvious ones that might not seem to have anything to do with revelation on the surface.

However, we must establish a few key principles that apply to this process. These principles involve those standard "Sunday School answers" or "Seminary answers" that we may gloss over quickly because we have heard them so much. Yet, oh, how vital they are in this process.

Tuning ourselves to the abundance of knowledge that God is pouring down from the heavens takes righteous efforts. If we learn how to better communicate with God through sincere prayer, then His communication with us will be easier to understand. If we increase our familiarity with His *written* word, then it often clarifies the words He *speaks* to us through the "still, small voice" (1 Nephi 17:35).

Heartfelt, consistent worship on the Sabbath and in holy temples is a personal investment in our relationship with Him; that investment, consequently, indicates we truly value what He has to say. Our obedience gives us the confidence to ask things we otherwise wouldn't. Repentance is a divine refining process of humility and accountability that brings us back to Him, again and again. Humility declutters our lives of worldly things so that His light can more easily penetrate through.

If we are not coming unto Christ in these and other ways to the best of our ability and knowledge, then, of course, personal revelation will be hindered. Indeed, we really cannot correct other aspects of revelation if these areas are still lacking. When we are making conscientious efforts in these areas already, and revelation still doesn't seem to be working, that is when we should begin to consider what else might be hindering it.

Get your notebook ready: The Spirit will be your real teacher. This next principle is a foundational concept I believe is essential to understand and incorporate in our lives when learning *anything,* but especially anything about revelation.

During my first year of teaching Seminary, one of my colleagues shared an experience with me that changed not only the way I saw my role as a teacher, but also as a student. He said that one day he had a strong impression that he needed to talk to Suzi,[23] one of his students in his next class.

However, when that next class period began, Suzi wasn't there. About 10 minutes into the class period, she slipped in through the back door and sat in the back corner. "Ok, good," he thought to himself. "I'll talk to her after class." However, just as he was finishing up his lesson, he saw her slip out early. He knew he would have to speak with her another day.

The following Monday morning, he heard a knock on his office door. It was Suzi.

"Oh Suzi," he said, "I'm so glad you came in. I've been meaning to talk to you."

"Well, actually, that's why I'm here," she said. "I just had to share something with you. Do you remember the lesson that you taught on Thursday on the Word of Wisdom? Well, I felt I needed to come and tell you it made a really big impact on me. And so I just wanted to thank you for it."

"Well, that's wonderful," this teacher responded, "but I didn't teach a lesson on the Word of Wisdom on Thursday."

And she said, "Yes, you did. Don't you remember I came in late to class and then I had to leave a little early?"

"I do," he said. "I remember you coming in late. I remember you leaving early. But I didn't teach a lesson on the Word of Wisdom on Thursday."

He said that Suzi then became visibly upset. "Yes, you did. And, because of what you taught, it changed some of the choices I made this last weekend."

As he started to say, "Do you want me to show you my lesson plan?" the Spirit simply said to him, "Be quiet . . . I taught her."

Elder David A. Bednar, while serving as President of BYU-Idaho, once encouraged students in a devotional to have a piece of paper and a pen handy. He explained, however, that it wasn't to write down anything *he* said but to pay attention to and write down the thoughts that would come to their minds and the feelings that would come to their hearts. "Listening to me is not important," he said, *"but paying attention to the promptings of the Holy Ghost is very important."*[24]

In all honesty, reading the words in this book isn't what's most important. However, listening to what the Spirit is teaching you is invaluable! In fact, the only way you will truly benefit from this experience is if you listen for what the Lord reveals to you about your situation and how you might be hindering revelation in *your* life.

Elder Richard G. Scott taught these divine impressions are "personalized instruction adapted to [our] individual needs by One who understands them perfectly."[25] That is because He understands *us* perfectly. When we are humble and willing, we can receive help from One who knows us better than we know ourselves.

This truth is also the reason I have not included a lot of specific answers or step-by-step solutions to the hindrances as you go through this book. For example, one hindrance to revelation we will talk about later is how we filter that revelation through false beliefs. When we unknowingly believe things that aren't true, those beliefs get in the way of the truths the Lord is giving us. Recognizing our false beliefs is a process that requires the Spirit's insight. I simply do not know all the beliefs you may have or the reasons for those beliefs. Changing those beliefs requires the Lord's help. Figuring out what we must do to make revelation flow better in our lives is a personal process.

As you listen for your own "Word of Wisdom Lessons," I also encourage you, as Elder Bednar taught, to continually write down what you receive. It's part of the reason there are blank lined pages at the end of each chapter — so that your experience with this book can become both personal and meaningful.

Elder Scott explained that when we write down the thoughts, insights, and impressions that God gives us, we signify to Him that they matter to us, that we deem them important, and that we desire to receive more. He also said, "If we fail to write down impressions, we can leave the most precious, personal direction of the Spirit unheard because [we] do not respond to, record, and apply the first promptings that come."[26]

Keep on the lookout for balancing principles. Lastly, I have discovered there are often balancing principles in the gospel — principles that steady our behavior or give us another way of looking at something. Elder Lynn G. Robbins even taught that many gospel principles come in pairs, meaning one is incomplete without the other. Some examples are agency and responsibility, mercy and justice, and faith and works.[27] This also seems to be true with certain principles of revelation. Let me share an experience that taught our family about this concept.

Years ago, one of our sons got a job that he quickly realized wasn't suited for him. The environment wasn't very good, and the sales tactics made him uncomfortable. Because of these conditions, he wanted to quit, but he was struggling to know if he should. One reason for his struggle was that our family motto has always been, "Hunsakers can do hard things. Hunsakers don't quit." This son had already had experiences in his life where he had lived by the principles of integrity, honesty, responsibility, and trustworthiness, and finishing something out even if it was difficult or unenjoyable. His commitment to that job also eliminated several other options that summer to help him to save for his mission — something that was important to him to do.

As he sought direction, he couldn't get an answer. When he first came to me for some insight, I felt I had an easy answer: "No, I think you need to stick it out." But as we continued to talk and my son shared more of his feelings, a different set of thoughts came into my mind: "There is a balancing principle here. Your son doesn't feel the environment of this job is good for him. He doesn't agree with the methods they use to sell the product. Both of those are also true and valid principles." With this added insight, my son decided to find a different job.

Throughout this book, we will talk about how revelation works and the principles upon which God governs revelation in our lives. As you learn, watch for balancing principles, or ideas that may steady, or even supplement, another idea.

You may find, for example, that sometimes one chapter will be talking about one way that God speaks to His children and then the very next chapter will talk about another, possibly opposite, way God speaks to His children. I've discovered there are many ways that God speaks to His children, each of them right. These different ways are not meant to cancel each other out, but simply to balance each other out, while bringing additional solutions to the table. The more we understand how revelation works, the more comfortable we will feel with the process, even if, and maybe especially when, it doesn't look like what we expected or what someone else is experiencing.

[1] "Revelation for the Church, Revelation for Our Lives," *Ensign*, May 2018, emphasis added; Elder Russell M. Nelson, "Stand as True Millennials," *Ensign*, October 2016, emphasis added: "Our Heavenly Father and His Son stand ready to respond to your questions through the ministering of the Holy Ghost."

[2] "Of Souls, Symbols, and Sacraments," BYU Devotional, January 12, 1988, emphasis added; "Personal Purity," *Ensign*, October 1998

[3] Elder Neal A. Maxwell: "Happily for us, brothers and sisters, the *vastness* of the Lord's creations is matched by the *personalness* of His purposes! . . . In the expansiveness of space, there is stunning *personalness*, for God knows and loves each of us! (see 1 Nephi 11:17) . . . . Think of it, brothers and sisters, even with their extensive longevity, stars are not immortal, but you are." ("Our Creator's Cosmos," *Church Educational System Religious Educators Conference on August 13, 2002, at Brigham Young University.*"); Elder Bruce R. McConkie also taught, "God is God because he is the embodiment of all faith and all power and all priesthood. The life he lives is named eternal life. And the extent to which we become like him is the extent to which we gain his faith, acquire his power, and exercise his priesthood. And when we have become him in the full and true sense, then we also shall have eternal life." ("The Doctrine of the Priesthood, *Ensign*, May 1982)

[4] President Boyd K, Packer, "Prayer and Promptings," *Ensign*, October 2009; "No Father would send His children off to a distant, dangerous land for a lifetime of testing where Lucifer was known to roam free without first providing them with a personal power of protection. He would also supply them with means to communicate with Him from Father to child and from child to Father."

[5] Elder Robert D. Hales, "The Holy Ghost," *Ensign*, May 2016; Sheri L. Dew, "We are Not Alone," *Ensign*, October 1998, emphasis added

[6] Elder Hales "The Holy Ghost," *Ensign*, May 2016

[7] Worldwide Leadership Training, February 2011

[8] Isaiah 55:8-9

[9] Moroni 7:48

[10] "The Voice of the Lord," BYU Devotional, December. 2, 1997

[11] "Did You Get the Right Message?" *Ensign*, May 2004

[12] "And Upon the Handmaids in Those Days Will I Pour Out My Spirit," *Ensign*, May 2010

[13] President Russell M. Nelson, "Revelation for the Church, Revelation for Our Lives," *Ensign*, May 2018

[14] Elder Patrick Kearon: "There can be no doubt that those with hearts carrying sin and unworthiness place barriers between God and themselves. Sometimes a heart can carry sin for so long that it becomes desensitized to spiritual things and incapable of receiving and feeling the messages of the Lord." ("Opening Our Hearts to Revelation," *Ensign,* August 2013)

[15] President Russell M. Nelson, "Stand as True Millennials," *Ensign*, October 2016; "Our Heavenly Father and His Son stand ready to respond to your questions through the ministering of the Holy Ghost. But it is up to you to learn how to qualify for and receive those answers."

[16] "Reverence Invites Revelation," *Ensign*, November 1991

[17] "Revelation for the Church, Revelation for Our Lives," *Ensign*, May 2018

BOXING THE LORD IN

[18] President Boyd K. Packer, "Reverence Invites Revelation," *Ensign*, November 1991

[19] "And Upon the Handmaids of the Lord," *Ensign*, May 2010; "Stand as True Millennials," *Ensign*, October 2016

[20] President Russell M. Nelson: "In like manner, what will your seeking open for you? What wisdom do you lack? What do you feel an urgent need to know or understand? Follow the example of the Prophet Joseph. Find a quiet place where you can regularly go. Humble yourself before God. Pour out your heart to your Heavenly Father. Turn to Him for answers and for comfort. Pray in the name of Jesus Christ about your concerns, your fears, your weaknesses—yes, the very longings of your heart. And then listen! Write the thoughts that come to your mind. Record your feelings and follow through with actions that you are prompted to take. As you repeat this process day after day, month after month, year after year, you will "grow into the principle of revelation" (*Teachings: Joseph Smith,* 132.)." ("Revelation for the Church, Revelation for Our Lives," *Ensign*, May 2018)

[21] "Opening Our Hearts to Revelation," *Ensign* August 2013

[22] CES Religious Educations Conference on the New Testament at BYU, Aug 8, 2000; adapted address found in the *Ensign*, "Teaching, Preaching, Healing," January 2003

[23] Unless otherwise noted, all the names in this book have been changed.

[24] "Teach Them to Understand," Ricks College Campus Education Week Devotional, June 4, 1998

[25] "How to Learn by the Spirit," *Ensign*, September 2014; emphasis added

[26] "To Acquire Spiritual Knowledge," *Ensign*, November 2009

[27] "Being 100 Percent Responsible," BYU Education Week Devotional, August 22, 2017

HINDRANCE #1

Boxing the Lord In

In the Old Testament, we learn about Naaman, the powerful commander who had delivered the Syrian army in a great battle. A respected man and natural leader, Naaman was held in high favor among many.

However, that doesn't seem to be why his story is in the scriptures. Naaman was a leper, and because his wife's handmaid knew of a prophet in Samaria, Naaman was part of an incredible miracle. The story leading up to that miracle is where we will begin our study about "boxing the Lord in."

Once Naaman discovered there was a way to be healed, he rode to Samaria with his chariots, a large sum of money, and, it seems, the beginnings of faith. However, when he got to the house of Elisha, the prophet did not come out to meet him. Instead, he sent out his servant, who told Naaman to go down and wash himself seven times in the river Jordan to become cleansed of his leprosy.

This angered Naaman, and he exclaimed, "Behold, I thought, He will surely come out to me, and stand, and call on the name of the Lord his God, and strike his hand over the place, and recover the leper. Are not Abana and Pharpar, rivers of Damascus, better than all the waters of Israel? may I not wash in them, and be clean? So, he turned and went away in a rage" (2 Kings 5:11-12).

Although there might be many reasons why Naaman was angered — including pride or misunderstanding or cultural tradition — there could be at least one other explanation: Naaman might have been upset because *nothing* in that experience ended up going the way he thought it should: "Elisha should have come out to meet me." "He was supposed to do something dramatic and perform a miracle right then." "Surely, he could have asked me to go bathe in some other river?"

In other words, Naaman had set parameters for how he was to be healed. He "boxed the Lord in." And because the Lord's help didn't fit in that box, Naaman wanted nothing to do with it.

Thankfully, we know that's not how the story ends. One of Naaman's servants was brave enough to ask him this important question: "Just because you didn't get the respect you thought you would, and just because this hasn't gone the way you thought it should, does that mean it is not of God?" It seems his servant didn't have a box for the answers to fit in. Naaman then chose to humble himself and went down into the Jordan seven times "according to the saying of the man of God: and his flesh came again like unto the flesh of a little child, and he was clean" (v. 14).

Naaman wanted to be healed of his leprosy. Yet, God seemed to have greater things in mind. He wanted to heal Naaman, not just of a skin disease, but of what was keeping Naaman from true joy and peace, even what was keeping Naaman from finding *Him*. So, He sent Naaman an answer that wasn't in his "box."

Sometimes, we carry around a similar box: a mental receptacle meant to receive the answers, help, or comfort we are seeking from the Lord. Our box, whether intentionally or not, sets the parameters of not only what He is supposed to do for us, but also how and when and where He is supposed to do it. We limit the Lord by "boxing Him in."

I find that we might not necessarily set these parameters because we think we know more than God. Instead, it might be because we think we know our specific situation better than He does, or at least that we, like Naaman, know what we want in that situation. However, when we *dictate* how revelation works in our lives, we can *diminish* what revelation we receive in our lives.

Let me share one time in my life when I boxed the Lord in. While in college, I decided early on that I wanted to be a marriage and family counselor. At the beginning of my junior year, I had narrowed down my graduate work to three schools that I wanted to attend and took the decision to the Lord several times, asking Him which of the three were right. However, for months I didn't get any real direction.

At one point, I had an Institute teacher pull me aside in the hall and say, "Stephen, have you ever thought about teaching Seminary?" I actually had. Right after my mission, I had spoken with the man in charge of the Seminary teaching program and, upon leaving his office, concluded that it probably wasn't for me. Besides, I had never imagined myself as a teacher. As I explained this to the Institute teacher, he simply said, "I understand, but still think about it, will you?"

About a week later, my former Seminary teacher, who had become a close friend to me, called me and said, "Hey, is there any way you could come and share a few thoughts with my Seminary class next week?" I wondered what was going on!

After teaching in his class that day, I again felt a prompting to talk to the administrator over Seminary, but I discounted the prompting because, in my mind, I already had a plan for my career (never mind that I wasn't getting any clear divine direction on my original plan!).

After more spiritual nudging, I finally decided to give it a chance and go through the application process. It required me to take a few classes, put some lesson plans together, and teach in front of my peers. However, I immediately ran into some roadblocks. I really wasn't very good at teaching. Plus, my heart really wasn't in it. Consequently, I began to come up with some very valid reasons why teaching Seminary as a career wasn't going to work. Thankfully, the Lord intervened . . . again.

I was invited to go teach a two-week trial class at a nearby high school. As I stood each day in front of those students — seeing their faces, hearing their stories, and sincerely hoping the lesson I had prepared that day was what they needed — something truly unexpected happened: My heart began to change. I fell in love with those students and with the rare opportunity a teacher has to bring light into others' lives.

I realize now that I had come before the Lord with a box and asked Him to give me an answer that fit in that box. I expected Him to help me choose from my pre-determined and pre-established list of possible outcomes: the graduate schools I had already researched, within a salary range I had already decided on, and among the job choices I had already considered.

I only wanted His guidance on options A or B or C, each of which was an ideal choice in my eyes. I didn't want an answer that wasn't in my box. I didn't realize that was what I was doing. Nevertheless, it was truly limiting my ability to grow, learn, and be guided during the experience.

However, as soon as I realized I had this box and started setting it aside, revelation began to flow. And as I continued to open my mind and heart to other options, revelation really began to flow — options that I had not thought of, expected, nor even wanted.

God started revealing to me not only what my next step should be, but also what He wanted me to do with my life. The prompting was clear: Choose another career outside of the marriage and family counseling arena; teach the youth and young single adults of the Church.

What I learned is that our Heavenly Father is always willing to give us direction if we are willing to seek Him diligently.[1] But sometimes, in our haste and eagerness, our seeking may sound like this:

- "Heavenly Father, I need an answer by Monday."
- "I'll accept any calling but . . ."
- "Lord, she needs to win this. Can you just please help her win."
- "I'll go where you want me to go, (dear Lord), as long as it doesn't require me to move to . . ."
- "Please don't tell me the answer is _____. I already know that. I need a different answer."

- "God, we'll have as many kids as you want, as long as it's not more than four."

We might also have expectations like these:

- "If I am supposed to switch majors, then I will know because _____ will happen."
- "If she is indeed the one, then I will know because _____ will happen."
- "If the Prophet is really a prophet, then when I go to Conference, I will immediately feel an overwhelming confirmation that he is the prophet when he walks into the room. I know this because my dad told me that, on his mission, the prophet visited the MTC. When he walked into the room, my dad immediately felt a confirmation in his whole body that he was standing in the room of a prophet."

Lastly, here's another way of looking at this; these are examples of "boxing" that I often use with the youth that I think we can adapt to apply to other circumstances, as well:

- "You can give me revelation in my patriarchal blessing, but not on the style, length, or tightness of my clothing."
- "You can give me revelation about which college to attend, but not if I should switch my schedule to fit Seminary in."
- "You can give me revelation about going on a mission, but not on what I should stop watching or listening to."
- "You can give me revelation during EFY, Girl's Camp, or Youth Conference but not when I'm hanging out with my friends, at a movie, or while at work."

In other words, "Lord, I really need Thy help and guidance, but You can only give me revelation if it fits within this box: my predetermined list of possible outcomes. You can only inspire me when I say I am ready for it or as long as it's already in my box. Please only answer my prayers if it's something I want to do or something I am good at. Otherwise, I just don't have time for it. I just can't do it. That just wouldn't work."

Elder Gerald N. Lund taught, "Sometimes, with the best of intentions, we inadvertently seek to tell the Lord how he should conduct his business. We may feel a great urgency about a question and press the Lord for an answer by a certain deadline. Or we may strongly desire a particular kind of manifestation, such as one of the more dramatic forms of revelation, and be satisfied with nothing less. We may try to tell the Lord how to solve our problems or what answer we would like. But these are not *our* choices. All aspects of the revelation are determined by the Lord."[2]

One time I had a college-aged young woman share with me that she was seriously considering marrying a phenomenal young man whom she was dating. He treated her like a gem, was diligently trying to be obedient and faithful in the gospel, and was working hard to pursue a career. He was a great young man. It was obvious he truly loved her. She even brought him home to meet her parents.

There was only one problem: her parents didn't think she should marry him. However, they were against the marriage because, in their family, they had discouraged their children from getting married before graduating from college. In fact, when this young woman asked if her parents had prayed about their opposition to a possible engagement, the mother abruptly said, "We don't need to pray about it. You know the rule in this house. If he's such a great guy, he can wait until you are graduated."

I didn't fully know the circumstance of this young woman nor the complete reasoning behind her parent's rule, but as she sat weeping in my office and asking me what she was supposed to do, I couldn't help but think of ways I may have done this same thing in different ways with my own children. Have I created a rule in our family that gets in the way of revelation? Have I been adamant that things are done a certain way, or in a certain timeframe, that has prevented the Lord from revealing to me a different or better way something should be done? We can box the Lord in with our own idea of timing, circumstance, or even the "traditions" of the way things are always done.[3]

Boxing the Lord in can also involve filling our box so full with our own desired answers or conclusions that there isn't much room for God's answers. Naaman headed to Samaria with a box already full of how he thought God would heal him and a list of ways that healing should occur. His faith was in what *he* thought the answers were.

We, too, sometimes go to the Lord thinking we are being open-minded, thinking we have the faith to accept any answer — but once we are given heavenly instruction, our first response sometimes is, "That *can't* be the answer." I had spent months praying for guidance about graduate school between choices A or B or C, when all along He was trying to tell me, "It's 'D,' Stephen. It's 'D,'" and I just wasn't open to that possibility.

What if the Lord tells us to simply show more love to that son whom we have already decided just needs more disciplining? What if our new calling *is* in the nursery? What if the Lord does ask us to have another child? What if the Lord *does* ask us to do "that"?

Years ago, my wife and I had an interesting experience with a job transfer. We were moving across the country to a very unfamiliar area. We knew what size of home we were looking for and where we wanted to live but soon discovered once we got there that we were in no way prepared for what the economy, housing market, schools, and neighborhoods were like.

Every day of our house-hunting trip, we kept having to change our criteria as we learned more about the area, moving farther and farther away from where I would work, and into "un-researched" places. Each night at the end of a long unsuccessful day, Michelle was usually in tears. Where were we supposed to live? It was a very frustrating and unsettling experience.

On our last day there, we still hadn't found a house. As we were on our way to another appointment, we happened to drive by a home that had a "For Sale" sign in the yard. We immediately stopped. Something felt very good about it. We knocked on the door to discover that it had not come up on our real estate listings because, up until a few hours before, it had been under contract. Their buyer had just pulled out.

From the moment we stepped into this house, we felt an immediate confirmation that it was a home that would work for our family. It was beautiful and in a great neighborhood that fed into great schools. We negotiated with the buyers to purchase it, flew home to pack our family, and arrived a few months later.

But here's the interesting twist to this story: Within a short time living there, we discovered that the cost of living in that area was much higher in ways we had not anticipated and that we could not afford to stay. About nine months later, we had to put that house up for sale.

As we began our house hunting again, we found ourselves being drawn to look in a wonderful community 15 minutes farther than our last house from my office, creating a commute of almost an hour. It was an area and size of home we never would have considered the first time around. We settled in and ended up loving that home and that new area just as much, living there for many years.

After that second move, I went through a period of time where I was frustrated with the Lord about the whole thing. Why hadn't He just led us there in the first place? It was not fun, to say the least, to pack everything we owned back up and move our family of seven *again,* changing wards, schools, friends, and neighborhoods. Months later, I was sitting in a priesthood meeting when a clear impression came to my mind: "This is where you were always supposed to be."

I realized that, because we had our own limited criteria of where we "could" live and what size of home we could live in, we wouldn't allow God to guide us to where we truly needed to be. In fact, each morning of that week looking for a house, we prayed earnestly that He would help us find the right place for our family, but it was a prayer asking for answers in the parameters we had set. He was kind and merciful enough to bless us in finding a great home in the meantime because I think He knew we wouldn't listen. It took us experiencing for ourselves the higher than anticipated cost of living before we would open our minds to other possibilities. And that was not God's fault. It was ours.

The prophet Moses was once given a grand vision of the lifespan of the earth and all God's children who ever had and ever would live on it. After many hours, he had been shown evidence through his spiritual eyes that "man is nothing," *something he "never had supposed"* (Moses 1:10-11; emphasis added). Sometimes God's higher and more holy answers fall somewhere out of our box simply because they are something we never had supposed.

Elder W. Craig Zwick tells of an experience he had as a Mission President with a young elder who announced the first day he arrived at the mission that he wanted to go home. Elder Zwick shared that he was sure, through long-suffering and encouragement, he could help this elder change his mind. Yet, after three agonizing weeks, the elder still wanted to go home.

Then, Elder Zwick said, "It finally occurred to me that I might not have the whole picture. It was then that I felt a prompting to ask him the question: 'Elder, what is hard for you?' What he said pierced my heart: 'President, I can't read.' The wise counsel that I thought was so important for him to hear was not at all relevant to his needs. What he needed most was for me to look beyond my hasty assessment and allow the Spirit to help me understand what was actually on this elder's mind. He needed me to see correctly and offer a reason to hope. Instead, I acted like a giant demolition wrecking ball. This valiant elder did learn to read and became a very pure disciple of Jesus Christ. . . . What a blessing it is when the Spirit of the Lord widens our view."[4]

With neither intention nor knowledge of doing so, Elder Zwick had essentially come to the Lord with an assumption of what that young man needed; he had boxed in the revelation for this elder. A single open-ended question removed that box, allowing the Lord to bless the lives of both men and probably countless others.

Sometimes what God is trying to teach us, or what the solution to a problem is, falls outside of the area of our understanding or expectations. God's higher ways always take into account things we don't know and cannot see. Just because that's where the revelation falls doesn't mean it's not from Him nor that it's wrong.

Indeed, President Ezra Taft Benson once taught that all "men and women who turn their lives over to God will discover . . . that He can make a lot more out of their lives than they can."[5] I have found that this making of our lives takes many forms. It involves expanding our vision, quickening our minds, and increasing our opportunities. Sometimes it involves divine direction that takes us places we never thought we would go or doing things we never thought we would do. It often includes options we never anticipated or experiences we never thought we would have. Yet, God's making of our lives can also mean we experience blessings greater than we ever thought possible — like Naaman's skin, which was not just restored to that of a seasoned warrior, but to the precious, beautiful skin of a little child.

If we will truly allow our Father to guide us — without parameters, without stipulations — He can and will guide us in ways we cannot even comprehend.

Lehi's son Jacob admonished his family to "despise not the revelations of God" and to "seek not to counsel the Lord, but to take counsel from his hand" (Jacob 4:8, 10). Let us despise not the revelation that comes to us outside of our box; let us seek not to counsel God in what choices we will consider. Let us set aside our boxes and make room for the greater, higher, sometimes unexpected, but always perfect, ways of the Lord. "For behold, we know that great and marvelous are the works of the Lord . . . unsearchable are the depths of the mysteries of him; and . . . he counseleth in wisdom, and in justice, and in great mercy, over all his works" (v. 8).

Therefore, What?

As you have learned a little bit better about the parameters of our role in relation to God's role in the revelatory process, have you recognized ways you might be boxing the Lord in? Have you realized times you may have been "waiting on the Lord" for a long time for an answer and it could have simply been because you were unwilling to accept a certain answer? Have you discovered an overflowing box that doesn't have any room for the Lord's answers?

Elder Neal A. Maxwell once asked this poignant question: "How can we sincerely pray to be an instrument in [the Lord's] hands if the instrument seeks to do the instructing?"[6] We can also ask ourselves some similar questions: "If I have parameters for the Lord, how guided do I really want to be? If I will only accept an answer that's already in my box, then do I honestly want an answer?"

Have I created a box? If you are unsure if you have created a box, consider Naaman's initial reaction to his unexpected situation: anger. Strong emotions — like anger, jealousy, frustration, fear, anxiety — can be an indication there's something slightly off . . . not with others or our situation or with God, *but with us.* Strong negative emotions can sometimes be a symptom of an unmet need or expectation. They are usually not the core issue, but a manifestation of the core issue.

Discover the "why" behind your boxes. As you recognize ways you might be boxing the Lord in, one way to begin removing them is to figure out *why* you are trying to limit God in the first place. That box didn't get there by accident. Is it the result of a fear or selfish desire that causes you to seek a certain answer? The "why" behind our behavior can not only tell us a lot about our behavior but also about ourselves.

For each of us, the reason may be different: one person may have a box because of pride, another may be setting parameters out of insecurity, and still, another might be resistant to the Lord's guidance because of lack of faith. It seems to me, however, that underlying all these reasons might be an issue of trust. We often box the Lord in because we struggle handing the decision completely over to Him. Or we are unwilling to consider the realm of His possible answers. When we begin to uncover the "why," it helps us figure out how to remove it.

Setting aside our box also involves submission. The more we want what He wants for us instead of what we want for us, the more our box can dissipate.

Boxing others in. Another aspect of boxing the Lord in is that we can also do it to others. We saw one way we do this in Elder Zwick's story. He had limited revelation for that elder because he thought he already knew what the problem was. I have discovered that I can also limit how the Lord can guide me in others behalf when I judge them. If I decide someone is full of themselves, that label severely limits what the Lord can reveal to me about them and for them. Will I be as apt to follow an impression to help a friend I have labeled as lazy? Will I show mercy to the young man in my ward I have judged as rebellious?

Will I hear the whisperings of the Spirit encouraging me to serve my teenager who has, in my eyes, been very ungrateful? Possibly not.

However, what we can also do is limit how others can help *us*. Sometimes when we seek counsel from our friends, family, or priesthood leaders, we expect their answers or help to fit in our box. Because of this expectation, their sincere efforts to help us can fall short of what, in our minds, should have happened — and sometimes regardless of how hard or sincerely they tried to meet our needs.

Consider a balancing principle. Lastly, an extremely important question you may be already asking yourself is this: How is boxing the Lord in different from making a decision among options and then taking that decision to the Lord for approval? We are counseled, as Elder Bruce R. McConkie explained, to learn to use the agency that God has given us to make our own decisions, reach conclusions that are sound and right, and then counsel with the Lord and get His ratifying seal of approval upon the conclusions we've reached.[7]

The caution, and I believe the difference between these two ideas, is that we just have to be careful on how set we are on our conclusions. As we follow that divine pattern — figuring out our options, making a decision, and praying about it — and decide to take Choice B to the Lord, we first have to be careful not to get really set on Choice B, but also to not limit the possible answer to only the choices we have considered. Maybe it's not only *not* B, but *it isn't A or C either.*

[1] D&C 109:7; Zephaniah 2:3

[2] "The Voice of the Lord," BYU Devotional, December 2, 1997

[3] D&C 93:39

[4] "Lord, Wilt Thou Cause That My Eyes Shall Be Opened," *Ensign*, November 2017

[5] President Ezra Taft Benson, "Jesus Christ – Gifts and Expectations," *Ensign*, December 1988; "Yes, men and women who turn their lives over to God will find out that he can make a lot more out of their lives than they can. He will deepen their joys, expand their vision, quicken their minds, strengthen their muscles, lift their spirits, multiply their blessings, increase their opportunities, comfort their souls, raise up friends, and pour out peace. Whoever will lose his life to God will find he has eternal life." (President Ezra Taft Benson, "Jesus Christ — Gifts and Expectations," *Ensign*, December 1988)

[6] "Willing to Submit," *Ensign*, May 1985

[7] "Agency or Inspiration — Which?" BYU Devotional, February 27, 1973

HINDRANCE #2

Being Recipe-Driven

A student of mine named Becca was having a cooking party with some of her Chinese friends. They were going to make some authentic Chinese food, and Becca was going to make them some authentic American food: chocolate chip cookies.

As she was carefully following her mom's tried and true chocolate chip cookie recipe, Becca's Chinese friend came over and, pointing to the piece of paper she was looking at, said, "Becca, what is that?"

"This?" she asked. "It's a recipe."

"What is a recipe?" he asked.

"It's the instructions I use to make my cookies."

"Do you always use one of those?"

She told him she did. And then he said to her, "Oh. In my country, we don't use those. We cook by feel."

"I thought that was interesting," Becca shared. "But I went back to making my cookies the way I always do — measuring everything carefully, leveling the flour with a knife, making sure I was adding the ingredients in the exact order they were listed on my recipe. I know that if I want my cookies to turn out like my Mom's, then I have to follow the recipe exactly.

"A moment later my friend came back over to me and asked, 'Can I ask you another question, Becca?'

"I said, 'Sure.'

"'Do you live your life that way, too?'

"I was so surprised at his question. But I found myself half-smiling and answering, 'Um . . . yeah . . . maybe I do.'"

Becca then shared with me, "As I thought later about his question, I realized that *is* how I live my life. I couldn't believe it. I want to be in control of everything, making sure I can control the outcome. I hate

29

surprises. And so, I plan things out in my life, 'measuring' everything carefully and in the exact order, trying to make sure that things happen exactly the way I want them to. And I do this all the time. I don't have a clue how to live 'by feel.'"

I've discovered that Becca's approach to life could be another reason we might struggle not only with certain aspects of life but also specifically with revelation. Sometimes, we try to live by a "recipe," much like we would carefully follow a recipe for chocolate chip cookies. I call it being "recipe-driven," and it usually involves this mentality: "If I do A then B then C, then surely I will get D." In other words, we expect that a certain investment of our time, energy, ability, or even faith will produce a certain outcome.

Similar in some ways to boxing the Lord in, this attitude hinders revelation in many ways. I've found either we aren't interested in God's input in our already perfected plan or we seek His sanction on our plan instead of seeking *His* plan for something in our lives. Thus, this attitude can also severely test our faith in Him — or at least what we *think* is faith.

The process of being recipe-driven might look a little different for each of us, but the premise is largely the same. We can be recipe-driven in relationships, jobs, and even callings. "I've got to be assistant manager by 28 and manager by 30, so I can take over the business at 35." We can create a recipe for gaining a testimony, repenting, or finding a spouse. "We have to visit all the church history sites so our children can gain a testimony of the Restoration."

Michelle and I have even recognized a recipe-like mentality in some of our parenting, thinking that there's only one path of success for a son, or only one acceptable outcome for our daughter. With this mindset, a parent's good intentions become a calculated effort to make sure a son is in baseball, student government, the honors society, and choir, or a daughter is popular, athletic, artistic, and spiritual — activities or character traits that almost become *checklists* for good parenting (or good kids).

One husband even shared with me: "I've figured out that somewhere in the back of my head I had a 'recipe' for a good marriage.

I had very specific 'ingredients' that I thought had to be part of a marriage. They were silly ideas like if we truly had a good marriage, then we would: discipline the same way, always be happy to see each other at the end of every day, or agree on how to invest our money. My wife and I have a great marriage, but often I have been frustrated with it without knowing why. I now realize it is because I thought that, without certain ingredients, my marriage wasn't good or would possibly fail."

Because I work a lot with college-aged young adults, I often hear this common YSA recipe: "The Perfect Start to Adult Life." (And to be honest, I think I had a similar recipe when I was their age.) Here are some of the ingredients I see in this recipe:

Step 1: Get into the college you've always wanted right out of high school and with scholarships

Step 2: Serve a full-time mission to your dream mission/come home just in time to start school

Step 3: Date a lot/have a great social life/live in the best apartment complex with the best ward/find perfect roommates

Step 4: Pick the "right" major the first time/never switch majors/never take unnecessary classes/i.e. never wander around wondering what you are going to do with your life

Step 5: Continue to get scholarships throughout college/never have financial struggles/never have to defer a semester to save money

Step 6: Have the perfect dating experience/never get your heart broken/ figure out early on that he/she is the "right" one

Step 7: Find that perfect person to date/court/marry your senior year so that you don't have to be "poor college students" the first year of marriage

Step 8: Get engaged in Spring, marry in Summer (because who wants to get married in the winter?)

Step 9: Start the exact job you wanted right out of college/quickly become successful in that job/have enough money to save up for a down payment on a home

Step 10: Buy a beautiful home on a great street in a charming neighborhood to start out your perfect life together

And what does that produce? *The perfect start to a perfect life.*

Maybe this sounds familiar to those of us looking back at that time in our lives. And maybe it's obvious now what the problem is with an equation like this: life just isn't about simply adding "ingredients" together in the right order to produce the results we want.

Our plans just don't always go as planned. We get sick on our missions and must come home. We can't figure out what to major in. We don't get the promotion we thought we would. Our children don't "turn out" according to our "recipe." Dozens of unwanted or unexpected ingredients that skew a recipe we are convinced is correct, or at least is expected of us. Even though we are taught that opposition is an integral component of mortality, we begin to wonder what we did wrong. After all, how can our lives really be good if every one of those things don't go exactly the way they are supposed to?

Can you see how being recipe-driven can cause problems in our lives? It's a very "me" centered, "my way" mentality that focuses far more on outcomes and outward successes than on experiences and the benefit of a process. We become so set on the way *we* think things should be done — on our "recipe" — that we don't want to consider another plan or that we might be wrong. In fact, there's really no room for any error in these recipes we create for life, which seems so contrary to the doctrine of the Atonement of Jesus Christ.

Moreover, recipes run contrary to the principles of divine revelation. In many ways, it often becomes an issue of commanding the Lord instead of commending ourselves unto Him. And I've found these recipes get in the way of revelation just as much with trivial things as with more important things.

For instance:

- How can we really be guided by the Spirit if we are so set that our daughter is going to be in a certain preschool?
- How can the Holy Ghost prompt us to go visit a neighbor if we are determined that today's recipe of getting the garage cleaned out is going to be fulfilled?
- Will we notice a teaching opportunity with our son if all we are focused on is that the bathroom sink gets fixed?

- Will we listen to impressions about other financial endeavors if all we are willing to focus on is getting out of debt?

But also, think about this:

- If taking over the family business has always been part of the plan, will we consider promptings about other paths?
- If we have set certain expectations on how a date should go, and it goes the exact opposite, will we be able to hear the Lord tell us to give that person another chance?
- If we have already figured out the one track to success for our daughter, will we listen when she wants to play the cello instead of play soccer? Or will *she* be able to hear the Spirit's guidance over our recipe?
- If we are sure that our son will only have a good experience on his mission if he gets called to the foreign country he has been dreaming about since he was young, will we be able to give him inspired counsel when he doesn't?
- If a death or tragedy "was not supposed to happen to our family," will we be able to feel the Lord's comfort or reassurance as we go through the anger and disappointment and feelings of betrayal?

In other words, our fear of or unwillingness to consider the Lord's "ingredients" hinders our ability to truly be guided and taught. There's not much room for the Lord's wisdom in our lives if we have already figured out all the ingredients we think we need, measured them carefully and exactly, added them in what we think is the perfect order, and are simply waiting to enjoy our finished product. There's not much room for His purposes or the miraculous manifestations of His grace.

If I am afraid of surprises, I might also be afraid of what God's ideas are for my circumstances. If I don't want anyone or anything interfering with my pursuit of the things I want, I might also resist letting Him into my plans. If I have an expectation of how the Lord should bless me for my righteous or conscientious efforts, I might also blame Him and distance myself from Him when He doesn't.

As I have studied and taught this concept of being recipe-driven, I've been reminded again and again of the rich, young ruler who approached Jesus. There are many principles we can learn from his story about sacrifice, consecration, or worldliness. However, there's also an incredible lesson in this story about how being recipe-driven can affect how we receive instruction from God.

From the various records of this story, it seems this young ruler was an obedient man; he knew the commandments and had kept them. When he came to the Savior with the question, "Master what shall I do that I may inherit eternal life?" maybe he thought he already knew what the answer would be, or at least he thought he had already done everything he needed to do (Mark 10:17). For when Jesus answered, "Go thy way, sell whatsoever thou hast, and give to the poor," the young man "was sad at the saying, and went away grieved: for he had great possessions" (vs. 21-22).

The Savior, as He does with every one of us, knew the young man's heart. The Lord gave him a personal instruction — even a *revelation,* if you will — of what he must do. But he couldn't follow it. Could it have been because the Savior added something the young man didn't want or expect, one that didn't fit in his "recipe"? Or was he upset because he had an expectation that his choices, his nice and shiny completed checklist perhaps, had already "earned" him eternal life? I have found in my own life that when unexpected inspiration comes, the closer I am tied to my "tried and true recipe," the harder it is for me to hear or accept that revelation.

Contrast the rich young man's response to that of Nephi when he was faithfully willing to "go and do" whatever it was the Lord commanded him to do.[1] Notice that faith and willingness wasn't because *Nephi* had figured out a way to get the brass plates, but because Nephi knew *the Lord* had prepared a way to get them.

The Lord's prepared way was probably not what Nephi would have planned if he had been given control of the situation. Indeed, he struggled with what, in the end, was the Lord's solution to the problem. But he handed over those decisions to the Lord, not knowing beforehand the things that he would do, and trusted in and followed the personal revelation God had prepared for him.[2]

That seems to be one of the dangers of being recipe-driven in regards to revelation: we become so confident, or at least anxiously tied to, our well thought out plan, we not only don't want the Lord slipping in any unexpected ingredients into it, but we want His stamp of approval on it. We, in a sense, might "pray about" what He thinks about our plan only because we are asking Him to *sanction* our plan. Yet, I've wondered: is it sincere prayer if I am simply asking God to make something happen exactly the way I want?[3]

It is very difficult to not want life to go just the way we like it all the time. It is hard for us humans not to try and organize fool-proof (and even trial-proof) plans. However, our plans could very well not be what is best for us. Indeed, there is, as President Henry B. Eyring taught, always "the possibility that we may have a selfish purpose that is less important to the Lord. For instance, I may want a good grade in a course, when He prefers that I learn how to work hard in the service of others. I may want a job because of the salary or the prestige when He wants me to work somewhere else to bless the life of someone I don't even know yet."[4] God's purposes are much bigger than ours. His definition of a blessing is much broader than ours, as well. And His guidance will reflect those purposes and definitions.

In this light, maybe being called to their dream mission isn't what will accomplish the refining that needs to take place in our missionary child's heart, even if we think it's what he or she needs or deserves. Maybe that means that some of us will suffer severe financial hardships even as we are trying to get out of debt. Maybe our perfect plans for our children's lives just might be limiting the lessons and experiences God wants them to have.

It might mean that not all of us will be a part of an ideal family, even as we are striving and hoping and praying and working for one.[5] Or that maybe a grueling battle with cancer can shape and change us and those we love in a way that nothing else could.[6]

When the Jaredites were divinely instructed to build barges to sail across the great waters, the Brother of Jared went to the Lord for guidance about three problems with those barges: light, air, and steering.[7] God took care of the air issue, let the Brother of Jared come up with a solution for the light issue on his own, and then left the steering problem unsolved. There was no steering wheel in those barges! And yet, the Jaredites boarded those vessels anyway, "and set forth into the sea, *commending themselves unto the Lord their God*".[8]

The Lord's plan for their journey happened to involve being driven by an incessant wind over mountainous waves, buried deep under a large body of water, and propelled through horrific storms for 344 days.[9] That doesn't sound very fun or very easy. In spite of this, those Jaredites shed tears of joy because of the multitude of God's tender mercies over them.[10]

Obviously, their faith was not based on a preconceived idea of how that trip was going to go. They trusted their God; they *commended* themselves unto Him in the beginning and continued to do so throughout their journey until they reached the promised land.

Elder David A. Bednar once shared a story about a young couple who exemplified an incredible example of this kind of commending instead of commanding. This couple had only been married three weeks when the husband was diagnosed with cancer and had asked Elder Bednar for a blessing. As he went to give the blessing, Elder Bednar explained he first asked them a question he "had not planned to ask and had never previously considered: '[John,] do you have the faith *not* to be healed?'"

Elder Bednar then continued: "In other words, John and Heather needed to overcome, through the Atonement of the Lord Jesus Christ, the 'natural man' tendency in all of us to demand impatiently and insist incessantly on the blessings we want and believe we deserve. We recognized a principle that applies to every devoted disciple: strong faith in the Savior is submissively accepting of His will and timing in our lives — even if the outcome is not what we hoped for or wanted."[11]

Becca's Chinese friends had learned to cook "by feel." I am not 100% sure what "living by feel" looks like, but I think it might involve some of this same freedom Elder Bednar taught about: liberating ourselves from the burden of always having to have the outcomes we want exactly the way we want them. Living by feel might be about focusing on what is in our power instead of trying to do what isn't.

Maybe it's about expending our energy exercising faith in the Lord's control over our lives instead of trying to control or manipulate the circumstances or people in our lives ourselves. It might also mean there are going to be surprises along the way, mistakes made, unwanted "ingredients," unexpected outcomes.

I think it might also involve redefining success, righteousness, happiness, or a host of other things. Yet, it seems certain that it involves seeking God's guidance for our journey and entrusting Him more with our journey by trusting His wisdom and purposes. In other words, it's much more about being led than always having to lead.

A student of mine recently shared this insight with me as she began to really apply this principle in her life: "As I started to realize that recipes are about what we want and not what God wants for us, it reminded me of the Savior in the Garden of Gethsemane. Instead of going by His own plan, Jesus said, "Not my will, by thine, be done" (Luke 22:42). Even when He was going through the hardest thing of all time, He trusted in the Father and followed His will. It made me realize that when I'm going through the hard times, instead of turning to my own 'recipe' and wanting *my* will to be done, I need to turn to the Lord and do *His* will. I believe that's how we will find true happiness in the end."

As we come to know our Heavenly Father better, we come to trust Him more. As that trust becomes more written in our hearts, we will find it easier to put off the natural-man tendency in us to want control over everything in our lives, including how the Lord directs our lives. In fact, as we gradually surrender our desires to His will and His wisdom like this, we won't need or even want the false security we feel when we try to be in control of everything.

We will also find greater ability to exercise faith in those things we don't have a perfect knowledge of, and those outcomes which are not seen, but which we know are true.[12] We will get better at trusting in the journey God has for us, even if, and maybe especially if, the process we had already figured out or the outcomes we were hoping for are not part of that journey.

Therefore, What?

As you begin to uncover some recipes in your life that are getting in the way of revelation, consider a few things:

Examine your expectations. An underlying factor in many of our recipes — as well as many of our disappointments, frustrations, and even struggles with faith in our lives — are our *expectations*: We *expect* our spouse to react a certain way. We *expect* a child to make a certain decision. We *expect* our conscientious efforts planning a family vacation to produce a perfect, stress-free, problem-free experience for every member of our family. These unwritten, often unspoken, ideas can get in the way of reason. They can get in the way of our relationships. And they can certainly get in the way of revelation — especially if our expectations about others are actually about *us*.

One mother shared an example of what this looks like:

"A few years ago when our oldest son came home from his mission, I found myself the first few days he was home feeling hurt, frustrated with my family, and even a little disappointed with my missionary. I couldn't figure out what was going on. It should have been such a glorious reunion. We were all so happy he was home. And yet I had all sorts of insecure emotions in my heart. I later realized that I had created expectations of the experience. I expected our reunion to go a certain way. I expected our son to act a certain way. I even expected our family to shape up a little bit and behave better than normal so that we could be one big happy family. And I didn't even know I had those expectations!

"However, because it wasn't quite happening the way I expected, I felt incredibly disappointed and frustrated with the whole experience. I also later recognized that because of those expectations, I was not as in tune as I could have been to what I might need to do or say to help our son transition after his mission the way he needed to. I was just hung up on what wasn't happening."

So, it is helpful to look honestly at our expectations. Often, we are unaware of what they really are. Take any upcoming event in your life or an endeavor you have devoted a lot of time or energy to. What are you expecting from it? What are you expecting others will do? Are your expectations of what someone should or shouldn't do for you, whether unrealistic or not, affecting your relationship with them? Also consider, how those expectations might be affecting your experience with revelation.

What are our expectations of the Lord? I've also noticed that, without realizing it, our recipes might also mislead us into thinking that certain righteous choices always lead to certain blessings from the Lord. Let me share several examples.

One family was surprised to find themselves struggling financially after their successful business of over thirty years started falling apart. In an effort to save their business, they used up all their savings and the equity in their home only to find, months later, that their situation had actually worsened and their debt had increased. About the time their business took a free fall, one of their brothers was also suddenly killed in an accident. It was a difficult and dark time for them.

A while later, this family sent their youngest son on a mission. The father then shared, "Surely, we thought, blessings were due to us. We were doing everything we knew how to do to contribute to the kingdom of God. . . . I began to wonder, 'Why is this happening to me? I'm a good member. I pay my tithing. I attend my meetings and serve in my callings. My son is serving a mission. Why isn't God supporting me in my righteous efforts? Where are the blessings that I should be harvesting? Why has everything gone so wrong when we have been trying so hard to do what is right?'"[13]

A dear friend of ours once shared with Michelle the heartache she was feeling because her son was choosing not to go on a mission. She was distraught — and rightfully so. But she was also confused: "I don't understand it. We have done everything right. We have gone to church. We have had family home evening. We have prayed and studied the scriptures as a family. I go to the temple often. He has gone to Young Men's and got his Eagle. Why did it not work?"

Another friend's husband unexpectedly decided to leave her and her children because of addiction, infidelity, and the desire to live a very different lifestyle. She wondered, "How could this have happened? We were doing everything we were supposed to be doing. This spiritual equation just doesn't add up."

I've heard many questions like these over the years. And I know Michelle and I have asked ourselves some similar questions from time to time throughout our lives. I don't pretend to know all the reasons these unexpected challenges happen nor why certain blessings don't come. However, as I've worked through these thoughts and questions, I've discovered that one reason we might find ourselves confused or full of doubt in these situations is that we misinterpret a familiar doctrine the Lord teaches in Section 82 of the Doctrine and Covenants. He says, "I, the Lord, am bound when ye do what I say; but when ye do not what I say, ye have no promise."

God promises that He is bound to bless us when we are obedient, faithful, and strive to do good. And I can testify that He truly does fulfill that promise. However, what we might misunderstand is that *He* is actually the one who usually decides what those specific blessings will be and when we will receive them.

He decides how He will bless us for sending a missionary out. *He* decides how He will bless us for paying tithing or attending the temple. He decides what blessings will come from conscientious and righteous efforts to do "all that we can" to qualify for them.

We may assume certain outcomes will be guaranteed because of our righteous choices, but, in reality, there's just a whole lot involved in this process that we cannot see or do not know. God's blessings usually seem to involve what will do us the most eternal good, not just "for-the-moment-good," which means sometimes He does not "bless" us by immediately taking away a burden or trial. In addition, it seems we can't be blessed in ways that take away the agency of others, nor does He always prevent others from making choices that will, in the end, prevent us from enjoying certain blessings.

This knowledge causes me to ask myself, "Do I really have the wisdom or perspective to know how the Lord should bless me or what my blessings should look like?" Elder Dallin H. Oaks once shared a powerful statement from a man who had just lost his teenage daughter to cancer that I believe sums up this principle so well: "Our family's faith is in Jesus Christ and is not dependent on outcomes."[14] I'm convinced that anytime our faith is in expected outcomes or the results of a recipe, we set ourselves up for struggle and disappointment.

So, going back to the expectations you started identifying:

- Do you have expectations of the Lord?
- Are you expecting Him to bless you a certain way?
- Are your expectations of Him influencing what you pray about and what answers to prayers you are waiting for?
- Could an expectation be the reason it is difficult to receive the guidance, reassurance, or even comfort from the Lord

that you need because it is something different than what the Lord is already giving you?

If you discover you can answer yes to any of these questions, one solution could be to re-define or even re-*calibrate* those expectations with doctrine by asking yourself: Is this expectation in line with what truths I know about God? Or revelation? Or prayer? Why do I feel this way? Is it because God blessed my neighbor like this and so I'm expecting the same? Is it because I believe I deserve it? If an expectation *is* grounded in doctrine, we can, with assurance, trust in it. If we are not sure, the journey to find out can be an incredibly enlightening one.

Analyze your definitions. Recipes also have a lot to do with definitions. Have you ever thought about what your definition of happiness or success or righteousness is? These definitions determine what ingredients we are expecting will be part of our lives. Until we know how we define success, we won't understand why we are pursuing a certain outcome or why we might feel like a failure. Until we understand how we define happiness, we won't understand why we feel disappointed or depressed.

For example, if one way I define righteousness is that all my children will marry in the temple, then what circumstances and people might I try to manipulate or control to produce that "righteousness"? What level of stress will I experience as my children grow up and move out? What will my faith be centered in — the Savior or the outcome?

I have found that the less our definitions resemble truth, the more likely we are to create a recipe to live by those definitions. However, the more our definitions are based on truth, the more likely we will be to approach situations, challenges, and even life in general with principles of truth like faith, trust, patience, humility, and gratitude.

Recognize the difference between recipes and goals. Whenever I teach this recipe-driven concept, a few usually struggle with the idea that it might imply we shouldn't make goals. Here are a few thoughts to help us understand the differences between recipes and goals.

In my mind, a true, realistic goal has at least three criteria. It does not try to:

- control or manipulate someone else's agency
- control elements that are out of our control
- control or influence the Lord's will

Using these criteria, it's not actually a goal to go on five dates this week. *Five girls must say yes.* Missionaries might make a "goal" to baptize five people in a month. However, "a missionary," Elder Dallin H. Oaks taught, "cannot baptize five persons this month without the agency and action of five other persons."[15] It's not really a goal to set our sights on being married by age 25, having five children, or becoming the CEO within five years. Each of these situations involves at least one element that is somewhat outside of our control.

True goals, on the other hand, involve *asking* five girls on a date or *inviting* five people to be baptized. They involve *trying* to be obedient, *working* hard in our career, or *exercising* more faith, regardless of how a human, or even the Lord, rewards us. They involve things that are truly within our power to control.

If you want to see how this works, take some time to write down a few of your goals. They can be any goals involving any facet of your life. How many of those goals are based on your agency alone? What part of a certain goal is possibly trying to work against the principle of opposition we are guaranteed will be a part of mortality? How many of those goals are actually trying to "bind" the Lord to bless you in certain ways?

Let's go back to the "goal" that all your children will marry in the temple. A righteous desire, for sure. However, it doesn't appear to be a doctrinally sound goal for it seems to go against the doctrine of agency and other factors that are out of your control. Instead, you can make a goal that, as a parent, you will take every opportunity to teach your children about the temple and the blessings of temple marriage, testify of its power and blessing in our lives, or go as regularly as you can and invite your children to go, as well. All that is within your power. With this kind of hope, your principle-based teaching and example will give them the greatest opportunity to use their agency.

If, perhaps, you are struggling to distinguish whether one of your goals is actually a recipe, watch for these feelings that arise, especially when a recipe doesn't seem to be working out. Do you . . .

- Feel incredibly frustrated, disappointed, or devastated about a setback
- Wonder what is wrong with you when you didn't make something happen
- Become angry with or blame God for failing to intervene in your life

- Find yourself tempted to manipulate circumstances or people to get your way
- Feel like you are not part of the "in group" that God blesses a lot
- Feel like a failure, even if other great things came out of an experience

_____

_____

_____

_____

_____

_____

_____

_____

_____

_____

_____

_____

_____

_____

_____

_____

_____

_____

_____

_____

_____

_____

_____

_____

_____

_____

_____

_____

_____

_____

_____

_____

_____

_____

_____

_____

_____

_____

_____

_____

_____

_____

_____

_____

_____

_____

---

[1] 1 Nephi 3:7
[2] 4:6
[3] "The object of prayer is not to change the will of God, but to secure for ourselves and for others blessings that God is already willing to grant, but that we must ask for in order to obtain." (Bible Dictionary, Prayer)
[4] "Gifts of the Spirit for Hard Times," *Ensign*, June 2007
[5] Elder Richard G. Scott, "First Things First," *Ensign*, May 2001
[6] "Stories of Faith," Kim White, www.thesmallseed.com
[7] Ether 2:19-20
[8] Ether 6:4
[9] vs. 5-8
[10] vs. 7-12
[11] "Accepting the Lord's Will and Timing," *Ensign*, August 2016
[12] Alma 32:21
[13] Tracy Hickman, "The Temple Stairs," *Ensign*, March 2013
[14] "Healing the Sick," *Ensign*, May 2010
[15] "Timing," *Ensign*, November 2003

HINDRANCE #3

Filtering Through False Beliefs

Many years ago, I met two young people who were obviously in love. Yet as I sat and talked with them one day in my office, the young woman told me, "I want to marry Jake[1] with everything in me. I love him. I've fasted. I took my decision to the Lord. And I've got my answer. The problem is . . . he won't marry me."

I was rather surprised by that statement. And so I asked Jake, "Do you love Katelyn?"

"Yes, I do. She's the most amazing person in the world."

"Do you want to marry her?"

"Yes, I do," he said, "but I won't."

Jake then explained to me, "When I was younger, I had a problem with pornography. I put my life in order and became worthy to serve a mission. After I got home, I had a couple struggles with it, but I am doing well now and feel there's been a lot of progress. But I just don't think it's fair for her to marry someone like me. I still have to fight to keep my thoughts pure. I just don't want to put her through this. She is such a wonderful girl, and so I just can't   marry her."

As we talked for the next hour, I shared with the two of them the doctrine of the Atonement of Jesus Christ and the power He has to heal and change us so that we're not in bondage to our past. We looked at the definition of the word "atonement," and talked about how it actually means "to cover" or to make "at-one" again.[2] We studied what Isaiah teaches about the Atonement, and how Christ has the ability to exchange our ashes (or lack of faith, or heavy burden, or serious sin, or whatever it is) and give us beauty and praise and righteousness and glory.[3]

I respected Jake's willingness to be accountable and responsible, and my intent wasn't to convince him he should marry Katelyn. I just wanted to make sure he understood the power the Savior had not only to forgive him, but also to heal and change him. As we talked, I could see some hope in both of their eyes. However, at the end of our conversation when I asked Jake how he felt, he said he was still struggling with the idea that he wasn't ever going to be worthy enough to marry her; he believed she deserved someone better than him.

After they left, I realized that perhaps the only way those two were ever going to be able to move forward in their relationship was if Jake figured out what he really believed about Jesus Christ, His Atonement, and what becomes of not only our *worthiness* but our *worth* to Him when we sin.[4] I felt he needed to figure out if he believed that redemption through Christ was truly offered to him and that it could actually help and heal him.

I knew Jake had a *knowledge* of the principles and doctrines about repentance, forgiveness, and divine worth. However, I also knew that he was struggling — not only to find peace through recovery, but also to receive a confirmation about making one of the most important decisions of his life. And it was largely because of a false belief that he would never be worthy to marry such an incredible young woman because of past sin.

I started this chapter with this story because it so accurately illustrates what I often see happen in the lives of the Saints: false beliefs getting in the way of revelation.

Although Jake's belief may not be your specific belief, our own false ideas can make it just as difficult to receive answers or confirmation or guidance in our lives. I have discovered that if our beliefs are unhealthy, unrealistic, destructive, or false in any way, the revelation we are trying to receive or act on is almost always affected.

To fully understand how these kinds of beliefs hinder revelation, we first need to understand a little bit better how our beliefs influence our lives in general. The way I like to teach this concept is to use the visual of a "belief box."[5]

Imagine that there is a place in our minds that holds the ideas we've been exposed to as well as the things we have learned and observed from the experiences we've had throughout our lives. We could call all of this our *knowledge.*[6]

In this space, however, we can also find our beliefs. Our *beliefs* seem to be the knowledge or ideas we have decided are *true*. In other words, we don't necessarily believe everything we know. For example, I might *know* that I have inherent worth that isn't dependent on anything temporal or temporary in my life, but what I might really *believe* is that much of my worth is actually connected to how good of a student I am or how much other's like me.

Thus, although there may be a lot of ideas, opinions, and philosophies floating around in our heads, only the ideas we have come to believe are true are the things that actually become our beliefs.

It could look something like this:

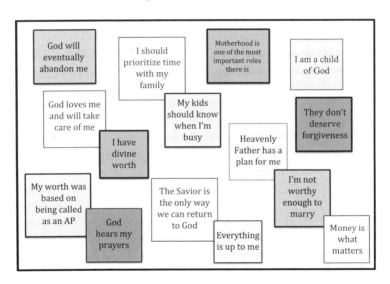

In this diagram, the ideas that are within somewhat transparent boxes represent our knowledge. Those that are in shaded boxes represent our beliefs. This is simply meant to illustrate that our beliefs usually become more fixed or "planted" than our knowledge in this space.[7]

Notice that not all the knowledge represented here is necessarily true, but it seems neither are all of the beliefs. Remember, our beliefs are simply the ideas we have decided are true. That means both the knowledge we possess and the beliefs we have formed from that knowledge can be healthy or unhealthy, realistic or unrealistic, positive or negative, godly or worldly, true or false.[8] Regardless of which one they are, if an idea has become our belief, we believe it is true!

Also, notice that some of the beliefs are in more darkly shaded boxes. That shading represents how some of our beliefs are more deeply ingrained in us than others. This could be because of the influence of others, the length of time we have believed them, extreme emotion related to a particular experience, or any number of things.

Now, if this box was actually a window we were looking through, our knowledge would be fairly easy to "see through." Although, it might be noticeable and somewhat influential on how we see ourselves, the world, or our relationship with God, it doesn't completely block our view. However, our beliefs would be much harder to ignore. They have much more of an influence on our perspective and perceptions. Thus, it seems, this "belief box" inside our heads isn't just a holding place.[9] It instead acts more like a *filter.*

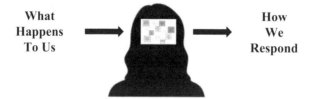

Consider the filters we add to a photograph on social media or a photo editing program. These filters change the picture's appearance by altering the shades of certain colors, making some parts brighter or more noticeable than before, adding contrast where contrast wasn't, and sometimes even distorting the picture completely. In short, they don't change the picture itself but rather how we see it.

So, too, do our beliefs affect the things we learn and experience. The conversations we hear, the interactions we have with others, the things we read, the environment we live in, the trials we endure — indeed most experiences we have pass through our beliefs and are influenced, altered, emphasized, or distorted by them in some way.

Furthermore, our beliefs also influence how we respond to those experiences. The choices we make, the things we think, and the emotions we feel are often directly affected by these beliefs, as well.

It could look like this:

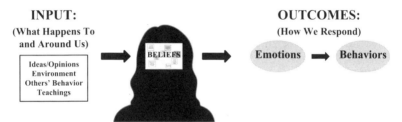

Why is any of this conversation important? Because the outcomes on the right are not solely determined by the things we experienced on the left, but often *by what they filtered through*. President Packer taught that "our behavior is not totally controlled by natural impulses. *Behavior begins with belief as well*."[10] This little "box" in our minds seems to be the lens through which we see life and, thus, it affects so much of how we feel, what we think, and what we say and do.

A quick real-life example shows how this works: Todd had an anger issue with his children. As he learned about this belief box concept, he asked himself, "Could it be that a false belief is at the root of some of my anger?" Upon digging a little, one thing he realized was that often he would get mad when his kids were bugging him when he was "busy" or asking him questions when they weren't "supposed to."

What did that really mean? He believed his endeavors were usually more important than their silly questions and that his kids should *know* when he didn't have time for them. But because children don't sense "being busy" the same way adults do, Todd's children were usually bugging him when he was doing something else or when it would be more difficult for him to answer a bunch of questions. This input would filter through his beliefs and result in anger, frustration, and unkind words and actions towards his kids.

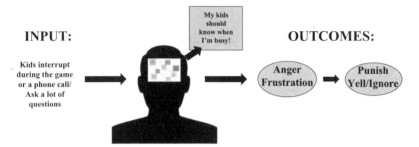

INPUT:

Kids interrupt during the game or a phone call/ Ask a lot of questions

My kids should know when I'm busy!

OUTCOMES:

Anger Frustration → Punish Yell/Ignore

In this light, it's possible that Todd's negative emotions or behavior towards his kids weren't necessarily because he didn't love them or wasn't good at parenting or was just a bad guy. Instead, they could have simply been because a few skewed ideas were influencing those interactions with his kids. This knowledge about his beliefs motivated Todd to do more digging to find out what other beliefs he had about his kids, his wife, his co-workers, friends, etc. that could be influencing how he felt towards them and treated them.

Now, there is much more to this concept than we have room for here — like the process of how our knowledge becomes a belief or how our beliefs become more deeply planted, to name a few. However, this is the basic idea. Our beliefs about ourselves, about the world around us, and about God and our relationship with Him really do play a part in just about everything we think, feel, say and do. They change the way we live our lives. They change the way we love. They influence our relationships. They affect the way we pursue an education or look for a job. They shape the way we pray or pay tithing. They impact the way we parent. They impact our faith.

As we really start to understand this concept, that understanding can change so much in our lives for it changes the way we see our lives. But possibly even more importantly, this understanding can change our experience with revelation.

An experience one young man named Luke shared with me begins to show us how:

"When I was quite young, my parents divorced and I rarely saw my father. Several years later my mother and stepfather also divorced. Then, I rarely saw my stepfather. I realize now that from those experiences I started to believe some incorrect ideas: marriages don't work and men leave you.

"As damaging as that belief was and is, it didn't stop there. As I continued through life, I transferred that belief to God: God is a man and so he's going to do the same thing to me — abandon me at some point. 'Why pray?' I thought. 'He doesn't love me.' 'He doesn't care about me,' I reasoned. 'He's just going to abandon me anyway.' Regardless of what I was taught about my Heavenly Father through those years, what I really believed was something very different, and my relationship with Him was definitely strained.

"I realize now that that was because whatever would come through the "box" in my mind, whatever experiences I had, the truths I was taught, even the impressions I would receive from the Spirit, would go through those beliefs and come out as anger, fear, defiance, and selfishness."

What we believe has just as much influence on our emotions, experiences, and choices as what happens to us — including our ability to receive, understand, and act on revelation.

REVELATION

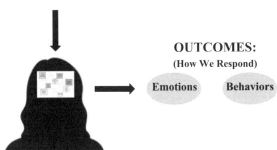

OUTCOMES:
(How We Respond)

Emotions   Behaviors

Revelation is an input, just like these other stimuli. And thus it seems we can filter the input of revelation through our beliefs, as well.

For instance, if we have a belief that we are just not as good as other people, that belief can weaken our confidence and ability to follow an impression to ask for a raise, be more open and vulnerable with our spouse, or accept a calling that stretches us. If we believe our in-laws don't like us, we will struggle when our spouse feels inspired to let them move in with us. If we believe that God likes to punish us or play games with our lives, that belief will greatly affect our ability to act on a revelation that pushes us out of our comfort zone. Even beliefs that are only slightly off can interfere with divine impressions by distorting guidance, limiting how much of God's love we feel, or even causing us to second-guess the first impression we received.

I had an experience on my mission where a false belief greatly hindered my ability to be taught, guided, and comforted by the Lord. And for a long time I wasn't even aware of it! It was a false idea that I realize now was planted the first day in the mission field.

An elder had met me at the train station. On the train ride to the mission home, this hardworking, dynamic, and obedient missionary immediately impressed me. He was so excited about missionary work and talked to everyone on the train that was awake (and maybe even a few who were asleep). He also happened to be one of the Assistants to the Mission President.

What I unknowingly started believing that day was that the definition of a truly good missionary was being just like this first missionary I met on my mission. In my mind, that must be how God showed approval to those who had truly served Him — call them as an Assistant to the Mission President.

However, although I worked diligently, lived obediently, and literally talked to everyone I met, I was never called as an Assistant.

With six months left of my mission, my Mission President called me into his office. Unaware of my feelings, he said he felt to share with me that he had been petitioning the Lord for some time to call me as his Assistant, but couldn't get a confirmation about it. He explained that he didn't fully understand why he was not supposed to call me, and that, in his eyes, I was trusted and worthy of it, but that he knew he had to be obedient to those impressions. I was completely confused.

I had an incredible experience on my mission, formed amazing relationships with many people, learned so much about myself, and really, honestly, gained a testimony of the Book of Mormon. (In fact, I can trace everything important and good in my life back to the foundations that were laid as I faithfully, diligently, and wholeheartedly served the Japanese people). But the disappointment of that experience permeated my soul.

It was especially evident on the twelve-hour plane ride home. Praying and pleading with my Heavenly Father to know if He had accepted my service, I couldn't seem to get a confirmation from Him. I couldn't find any peace. In fact, it seemed that at that moment I couldn't feel *anything* from the heavens. I even began questioning if He approved of me or if I had done *any* good on my mission at all.

All of this might sound crazy to you . . . or maybe it doesn't. (To be honest, it's not easy to share such skewed thinking.) However, that experience has continued to teach me many valuable lessons throughout my life. And it has especially taught me about the power of our beliefs and the influence our negative or false beliefs can have not only on revelation but on our relationship with a loving Heavenly Father who so badly wants us to feel and know of His love.

That false, worldly belief about position that I had turned into a "gospel truth" influenced how I saw, felt about, and understood many things. I was somewhat blinded by what mattered most to the Lord. My narrow definition of God's approval made it hard for me to learn *His* definition. I had a hard time seeing the *real* evidence that I was becoming a disciple of Jesus Christ: things like the changes in myself or the growth in my testimony.

In fact, from the last six months of my mission until many years after I got home, I struggled to feel the ministering of His peace or hear the messages of His approval. Revelation seemed to flow in other aspects of my life, but when it came to my worth being connected to a position, I struggled because of those false beliefs.

Over the years the Lord was able to tutor me. Yet, sometime later something President Dieter F. Uchtdorf shared gave me added understanding and peace. He explained that as he would go to reorganize stakes around the world, sometimes a brother would surprisingly share that he had received an impression about being in the next Presidency. President Uchtdorf said that when he first heard this, he wasn't sure what to think. But over time, the Spirit taught him this: "Sometimes [the Lord] grants spiritual promptings telling us that we are worthy to receive certain callings. This is a spiritual blessing, a tender mercy from God. But sometimes we do not hear the rest of what the Lord is telling us. 'Although you are worthy to serve in this position,' He may say, '*This is not my calling for you.* It is my desire instead that you lift where you stand.'"[11]

Knowing this truth probably would have helped me when I was a young missionary in Japan. I wonder if I was so disappointed at what *wasn't* happening in terms of callings and positions that I wasn't able to hear the Lord tell me, "You are worthy of it, Elder Hunsaker. Your President confirmed that. . . . I just need you *elsewhere*."

How open will the conduits of heaven be in our lives when we incorrectly define the help that will come through those conduits? How difficult will it be to feel the comforting witness of God's love when we have narrow beliefs about what His love looks like? How will we feel God's approval or confirmation when disappointment is completely blocking the Lord's influence — a disappointment, no less, that is completely founded on a false expectation?[12]

Our false beliefs can also affect our willingness to follow an impression to do something we weren't planning on doing, something we've never done, or even something that we don't really want to do.

Think about the story of Jonah. He was instructed by the Lord to go to Nineveh to warn the people they were going to be destroyed if they did not repent of their wickedness. But instead of being obedient, Jonah ran as fast as he could to the coastal city of Joppa, found a ship going to Tarshish, and sailed as far away from his responsibility as possible.[13]

Have you ever wondered why? At first, we might think that Jonah was afraid. Or maybe he just didn't like calling people to repentance. Yet, it seems it was so much more than that.

Jonah had somewhat of a history with the Ninevites. They were a powerful, idolatrous, and barbaric people who had enslaved, tortured, and killed Jonah's people over a long period of time. It might be safe to say that Jonah probably didn't like them.

And so, when the revelation came, Jonah probably had some pretty strong beliefs about the Ninevites. That revelation probably filtered through those beliefs, not only affecting his attitude towards that revelation, but also affecting his obedience to it.

Later in Jonah's story, when that great fish spit him out on the shore and the Lord told him a second time to go to Nineveh, Jonah was compelled to obey. But it doesn't seem like he had changed what he *believed* about the Ninevites. He preached unto them and then sat down and waited for them to be destroyed, even though they had turned "every one from his evil way, and from the violence that [was] in their hands," and began to believe in God (Jonah 3:5, 8).

When the Ninevites weren't destroyed, Jonah was angry that God hadn't done what He originally said He was going to do. He believed the Ninevites deserved to be destroyed even though they had started to repent; it seems he didn't think they deserved mercy. It is interesting to point out, however, that it wasn't the revelation for Jonah to minister among the Ninevites that was the problem, nor how God handled their rebellion. It was Jonah's belief about the Ninevites that negatively influenced his emotions and behavior.

We probably won't receive a revelation to go to Nineveh. Instead, we might receive an impression, "Forgive your dad." That revelation might immediately filter through the belief, "But my dad doesn't deserve forgiveness" or "I could never forgive my dad" or "Forgiveness means forgetting or condoning what happened." And then we might become angry that God would ask us to do something like that and run, like Jonah, as far away from the revelation as we can.

Again, the revelation itself isn't what's wrong in this situation, even if it feels like it. The negative feelings we might have or the temptation we might feel to disregard it could instead be caused by a negative, unhealthy, or false belief.[14]

What if we have a belief that when God gives us a divine revelation from on high, then everything associated with that revelation is going to "work out." And what if for one person, the definition of "work out" means that if God inspires them to put their house up for sale, *then they will actually sell it*, or that if God tells them to start looking for another job, *then they will actually get the new job they really want*. These kinds of false ideas actually cause us to expect that following divine instruction means the Lord will pave an unobstructed path of gold to the end destination of that revelation. And when that path of gold never appears, we might begin to doubt Him and His genuine concern for us, or we might even doubt the revelation, *but usually not the false idea*.

As a parent, a belief that I am always right — or that I have to be right otherwise I am weak or incapable — can negatively affect so many aspects of my relationships with my children. A belief that I'm only a good parent if I'm always liked by my children will surprisingly do the same. However, both of these beliefs will surely also interfere with my ability to receive and act on revelation in this role. How likely will I be able to hear the Spirit direct me to do something I don't think is the solution? How difficult will it be for me to hear the Spirit tell me I'm wrong about the way I handled a situation with one of my children? How easily will I receive, or more importantly follow, inspiration that I know will upset my child?

These are just a few examples. There are so many ways false beliefs can get in the way of revelation. Hopefully, you've been able to begin to recognize some of your own beliefs that may be hindering revelation in your life. As you do recognize them, be assured that the solution to this challenge is not complicated: False or unhealthy or unrealistic beliefs can be changed. And when they are, our experience with revelation will automatically change, as well.

We'll talk more about *how* at the end of this chapter, but here's one example: A friend of mine had had some difficult challenges with a few of his children. One day as he was kneeling down to plead for the Lord's help with one of them, the words that he felt to say were, "Heavenly Father, wilt thou please bless *our* child." At that moment, he realized that he had believed this child was only his responsibility and problem. He knew the doctrine, but what he honestly believed was that he was supposed to somehow fix everything and know all the answers. That one inspired phrase, words given him "in the very hour" that he needed them (D&C 100:6), changed everything. It shifted his thinking and replaced a false idea with completely true doctrine, changing his prayers, his hope, his relationship with his children, and his ability to receive further guidance for his children.

As we correct our false, unrealistic, destructive, or unhealthy beliefs with truth — and as we make sure we actually *believe* those truths — revelation will flow with much more clarity in our lives. Revelation always flows with power and simplicity when it flows through truth. It isn't bogged down by fear or misunderstanding or false definitions or lies or any other encumbering thing.

Going back to Jake and Katelyn's situation, I didn't see them after our first conversation for several months. Then one day I walked up to my office and found, sticking out of the bottom of the door, an envelope. It was a wedding invitation.

As I opened the door, I could see the envelope flap was unsealed and open. Looking closer, I saw these words written across the top: "Because of the Atonement." I then pulled out the invitation to see their smiling faces moving forward in faith and trust in their God.

Through the redeeming and enabling power of Jesus Christ, Jake was able to change some of his beliefs, which ended up changing the entire trajectory of his life. He came to believe with more surety that the promises made to all were also made to him: that the great exchange between scarlet and snow and crimson and wool is real.[15]

As his beliefs were corrected, the barriers Jake had erected between him and God slowly began to come down, giving him the courage and ability to turn to Him and allowing the light of His love, approval, strength, and inspiration that had always been there to pour into his life. It was truly a miracle.

Because of the Savior's Atonement, the same thing can happen for each one of us. We do not have to endure the bondage that false beliefs create, nor do we have to remain in a shuttered room where God's light cannot reach us. Because of the Savior's Atonement, we can become free and more freely enjoy the flow of revelation in our lives.

Therefore, What?

This concept about the role that our beliefs play in everyday experiences is an important one to understand. Not only will it make a difference in those everyday experiences, but it will also make a significant difference in our revelatory experiences.

Now that you might have a little better understanding of it, let's first figure out what we believe, then we'll talk about how we change and correct our false beliefs. You might want to get comfortable, though. This *"Therefore, What?"* section has more homework than usual, and it's only because it's so necessary and so helpful. The more we understand what our beliefs really are and how to correct them, the more often our daily revelation will filter through truth.

What do I truly believe? A great way to begin to figure out what beliefs we have is to start noticing what things in your life trigger strong emotion or negative behavior. Remember, our emotions and behavior are usually the outward evidence of something going on underneath, much like a headache is often simply a manifestation of something going on deeper in our bodies.

Start by asking yourself questions like these:

- What situations or choices of others make me angry?
- What makes me jealous or sad?
- What situations tempt me to lie or be rude to someone?
- Why am I afraid to ask for time off at work or for help from a neighbor?
- Why does that commandment frustrate me?

Often, we will discover that unrealistic or unhealthy beliefs are at the root of these feelings. In fact, I have found it is often not our negative *experiences* that hold us hostage. Instead, it seems to be whatever beliefs we formed because of those experiences that do — beliefs that consequently have the power to influence every new experience for years to come.

Notice, also, which experiences *specifically with revelation* cause negative emotions or behavior. Sometimes if a revelation causes us stress, we may think, "Oh maybe that was just me" or "Maybe that wasn't revelation." However, if we feel angry, depressed, stressed, or frustrated because of a revelation, it is possible that the revelation is not the problem, but rather the false idea it is filtering through. Just as Elder Dieter F. Uchtdorf counseled us to first "doubt our doubts" before we doubt our faith, I believe we must first question our negative feelings about a revelation before we doubt the revelation.[16]

Start a Belief Inventory. Another effective way to find out what our beliefs are is to make a "Belief Inventory." This inventory involves actually writing down what you believe about God, yourself, and the world around you.

One way to do this is to get three different pieces of paper and write "What do I believe about God?" at the top of one, "What do I believe about myself?" on the next one, and "What do I believe about the world around me?" on the last one. Then, start writing whatever comes to mind as you try to figure out what you honestly believe about each one of those things, not just what you are supposed to believe.

Here are some questions that might help get you started:

- What do I genuinely believe about myself?
- How do I see myself?
- What do I expect from myself?
- How do I define a "good person" or a "successful person"?
- What do I expect from the people in my life?
- How do I see the world and others around me?
- What does the world expect of me?
- What kind of a God is the God I believe in?
- How do I see Him?
- What are His characteristics and attributes?

- How does He bless or reward His children?
- What are my Heavenly Father's expectations of me? And how do I feel about those expectations?
- What are my expectations of Him?
- How do I define "righteousness"?

As you begin this process, it may be difficult at first. A few ideas may come, and then nothing. Or you may jump from one topic to the next. It can take you several days, weeks, or months to figure things out. (Michelle and I are still discovering false beliefs we didn't know we had years into this process.) Just keep working at it. These might be things you haven't thought about deeply, and they take some excavating. So make sure you dedicate some time to sit down and write — without anyone reading what you are writing and without censorship.

In fact, as you go to write something, if you start thinking, "Oh, boy, I probably shouldn't write that," write it anyway — even if it is something you "shouldn't" believe. God already knows you believe it. This exercise is meant to get in front of you, in writing if necessary, things in your mind that *you* might not be aware are there. We can't change something we don't know is there.

And don't be surprised that you find some really incorrect beliefs hanging out in your head. I've discovered that it is almost impossible to not have some of this world rub off on us as we live in it every day — just like it's impossible to go camping and not get at least some dirt on us somewhere.

The adversary is also working full time to make sure this contamination happens. I think of man's first experience with Satan on this earth. The very first thing he did was try to distort the truth that Eve had been taught by the Father about eating the fruit of the tree of knowledge of good and evil.[17] Shortly after, he stepped in and told Adam and Eve's children to "believe not" what their parents had taught them about the power of knowing good from evil, the joy of their redemption through Christ, and the promise of eternal life. And they did exactly what the adversary suggested and "believed it not" (Moses 5:13). Part of the battle of this mortal experience is whether we will plant truth or untruth in our minds and hearts.

Here are a few realizations others have discovered from this going through this process of figuring out their beliefs:

"Almost all my beliefs about God were somewhat true, but my beliefs about myself were almost completely negative and wrong."

"I realized I don't really believe in miracles."

"I discovered I have a terribly negative view of the world and others around me, believing all sorts of things that make me angry and frustrated with life."

"I actually prayed one time after working on this list for a while, 'What false beliefs do I have about Thee?' Within a short time, this thought came to my mind: sometimes I don't want to pray to Him because I feel like He's upset with me. I didn't know I believed that. And I didn't know why I believed that. But I realized it was a pattern that had happened many times in my life."

"The beliefs I have about my children are almost a direct reflection of the beliefs I have of myself — nothing they do is good enough, yet neither is anything I ever do good enough in my mind. But here's what's crazy. I think that's because I don't think anything I do is good enough for God. I feel like He's always disappointed in me."

That last comment leads us to one last thought on our Belief Inventory. It is not a coincidence that I suggested you start with what you belief about God first, then yourself, and then others. I have discovered that what we believe about God is usually at the core of what we believe about everything else in our lives. And this seems to be true even if we don't like God, want Him to have anything to do with our lives, or even really believe in Him. Our beliefs about, or lack of belief in, a heavenly being seem to influence almost every perception we have, even if we don't realize it. This could be, at least in part, because, as the Prophet Joseph once taught, "if men do not comprehend the character of God, they do not comprehend themselves."[18]

This discovery has become even more evident as I have counseled others over the years. Time and again, their struggles often boil down to what they do or don't believe about God. Some may be convinced they struggle because of low self-esteem or lack of motivation or anger — things that seem to have to do with personal character flaws. Or they believe they struggle because of how others have treated them. Yet, when they really do some digging, they sometimes discover they struggle because of an incorrect belief about how *God* feels about them — or in other words, what He expects of them, how He values their efforts, how much He cares about them, or what His love is based on. We often project what we believe about God to ourselves. And we often project what we believe about ourselves to others. But the whole cycle usually starts with our beliefs associated with God.

It seems this could also be one reason the Savior taught that the first and greatest commandment was to "love the Lord thy God with all thy heart, and with all thy soul, and with all thy mind" (Matthew 22:37). It is first because it seems that until we can do that, we cannot really love others or ourselves. I've found that as we come to love God and correct our false beliefs about Him, we will come to love ourselves and correct our false beliefs about ourselves. This love will then help us to love others and correct our false beliefs about them.[19]

Fight false beliefs with truth. So, how do we get rid of our false beliefs once we realize we have them? Recognition is definitely a huge first step. Some have even shared with me that simply realizing a false belief was at the root of a problem has made the belief almost melt away — and thus often the problem! Others experience relief when they realize that they, themselves, are not flawed or ridiculous, but simply that their beliefs are. There is power in recognition and, hopefully, this power has already blessed your life as you've progressed through this book.

Once uncovered, false ideas can be also corrected as they are held up next to truth. I have seen it happen often enough to know that anything that is truth has the power to correct anything that is false, no matter what kind of "false" it is! In fact, I love how one brother explained it in his testimony: "Truth has the power to soften the roots of things that are false, making them weak and easy to remove from our lives."[20]

In the same talk that President Packer taught that behavior begins with belief, he also gave us this precious, and probably familiar, truth: "True doctrine, understood, changes attitudes and behavior. The study of the doctrines of the gospel will improve behavior quicker than a study of behavior will improve behavior. . . . That is why we stress so forcefully the study of the doctrines of the gospel.[21]

In light of what we have been talking about here concerning beliefs, I have found that true doctrine, when understood, truly does correct attitudes and behavior. And it seems to be at least in part because our false beliefs become corrected by that doctrine in the process — which then influences our attitudes and behavior.

As you discover false beliefs in your life, ask yourself, "What true doctrine, if I understood better, would correct the false idea I have?" "What attribute of the Savior, if better understood, would change what I believe about my son?" "What false doctrine is causing me to have this expectation of myself?" "What don't I really understand that is causing me to not trust the Lord or to be angry with Him?"

For example, think about the belief "My dad doesn't deserve forgiveness." What doctrine of the gospel teaches us why that belief really can't be true? Further, what doctrine might we *know* but we don't actually *believe*? We may hear and learn and "know" a lot of things, but what we know and what we actually believe can be two different things.

Elder Bednar once taught: "I am acquainted with Church members who accept as true the doctrine and principles contained in the scriptures and proclaimed from this pulpit. And yet they have a hard time believing those gospel truths apply specifically in their lives and to their circumstances. They seem to have faith in the Savior, but they do not believe His promised blessings are available to them or can operate in their lives. . . . We often testify of what we know to be true, but perhaps the more relevant question for each of us is whether we believe what we know."[22]

Facing the truth. What if we discover some of our negative beliefs are true or have some truth to them? "I'm really not very good at this." "She is constantly tearing me down." "I'm really lazy, especially when it's something I don't want to do." "I can't believe I did that. I'm so pathetic." I believe the same principle we talked about before applies here. We must hold these ideas up to eternal truth, as well.

Maybe we really aren't very good at something. But truth tells us that inadequacy doesn't change our worth. Maybe someone else is constantly belittling us. Truth tells us that what others think of us is not the final judgement of us. It tells us when we must distance ourselves from someone. It also tells us that we can even be given the power to love those who mistreat us instead of being debilitated by them.

Maybe it's true we don't work very hard in certain situations. Or that we really shouldn't have done something we did. But what about the belief that we're lazy or pathetic helps us find the motivation to change? Nothing. Truth tells us that laziness or even sin doesn't inherently make us bad people. Truth helps us find hope that, through the Atonement of Jesus Christ, we can be forgiven and strengthened in our weakness. So, maybe one really important thing we can ask ourselves when a negative thought is dominating our life — true or not — is "Is this helpful? Does this motivate me to do good or change?"

Label the belief. Once we have recognized that we have an incorrect belief or unrealistic expectation of ourselves or others, we can also call it what it is. For example, any time we react negatively to an experience, we can say: "This is my 'perfectionist belief' coming through;" or "This is my 'everything works out for everyone else, but nothing works out for me belief' playing right now;" or "I am feeling this way because of an incorrect belief, not because no one cares about me." One sister even chooses to say to herself: "No matter how true this idea may seem, I know it isn't *truth*." When we actually give these thoughts a label, it can often take away some of their power and help us see things more clearly.[23]

How big of a tree will we need to cut down? There's one last thing to understand once we have recognized a false belief. It is helpful to figure out where the false idea came from — not to blame our parents or dig up the past, but simply to know just how big of a tree we are going to have to cut down and how long it will take us to do it. Usually the longer we have had them, the more rooted our beliefs are. It also seems the more intense or extreme the experience, the deeper the belief goes, whether good or bad.

In my own experience, some of my beliefs were planted so long ago, they are a towering oak. They just are not going to go away with one heartfelt prayer tonight before I go to bed. Sometimes, some beliefs melt away almost instantly, even if we have held on to them for many years. However, often they take weeks, months, even possibly years to dissect and correct.

For example, one sister I know had long held unrealistic expectations of herself that eventually began contaminating nearly every experience she had. Once she began recognizing them, she exercised faith in Jesus Christ and His ability to correct those beliefs through prayer, studying His word, fasting, seeking priesthood blessings, and attending the temple. She talked through her tangled web of beliefs with her husband and close friends, asking them to continually remind her of truth. After several years, she was able to correct those beliefs — one day at a time, one prayer at a time, slowly but surely. She was truly able to let them go and heal from the damage they had caused her.

The process isn't the same for everyone nor in similar situations because it's a very individual journey based on agency, faith, the Lord's divine customization, and a host of other things. However, I know that each one of us can be freed from the bondage of false beliefs.

Focus on the Savior. Regardless of the approach used, faith in the Savior and His healing, redeeming, and enabling power must be part of the process.[24] Even though having an incorrect belief or an unrealistic expectation of ourselves is not the same has having sinned, we still need Christ's power to change it and exchange it for truth. I just don't think we can change *anything* within us completely by our own power, regardless of what it is. As mentioned before, some of our beliefs are so deeply ingrained in our minds, they can silently influence everything, and without our even knowing it. We must have divine help to untangle that kind of a web.

Knowing this, the heartfelt pleading from the father of the child with the unclean spirit takes on more meaning: "Lord, I believe; *help thou mine unbelief*" (Mark 9:24). Our own pleading may look something like this: "Lord, I truly do believe in Thee and thy power and mercy and love. I know that Thou can do miraculous things. Please, please help me with what I don't really believe in. Please help me to see where I have things wrong. Please change in me the beliefs that are not true about Thee. And please help me to have hope as I wait for these things to be corrected in me and to have the necessary faith as Thou mends the hearts and the relationships I have hurt in the process."

Knowing what to focus on. One really exciting outcome of correcting our false beliefs is that we are able to get to the root of change. I've noticed that if people want to change their behavior, they usually focus on their behavior: if I'm really not good at reading my scriptures consistently, I might focus on changing the time of day I read or I might try to get up earlier so I actually have time to read them.

Similarly, when people want to change their emotional reaction to something, they usually focus on changing that emotion: if I am the father in this chapter who is often getting mad at his kids, I might focus on loving my children more or trying to be more patient.

But what often happens in either case? Two weeks later (if it takes me that long), I'm back to doing the same thing — I'm not reading my scriptures consistently or I'm getting upset with my kids again over little things. Why does this happen? Because, fundamentally, my *belief* hasn't changed in either of those situations.

Similarly, we might, in an effort to change, focus instead on the stimuli in our lives: "That roommate is always bugging me; I need to find a new apartment." "I hate this job/boss/work environment; I need to find a new job." "I need to stay away from the kids when I'm overloaded with concerns about work."

And what often happens? My new roommate is just as annoying, my new job stinks just as much as the last one, or I find myself spending more and more time locked up in my den. Why? Because my belief about each of those things hasn't changed.

Remember this profound truth from President Ezra Taft Benson? "The Lord works from the inside out. The world works from the outside in. The world would take people out of the slums. Christ takes the slums out of people, and then they take themselves out of the slums. The world would mold men by changing their environment. Christ changes men, who then change their environment. The world would shape human behavior, but Christ can change human nature."[25]

It seems true, long-lasting change is rarely found in focusing on the external elements in our lives — meaning not only our environment, but our emotions or our behavior, as well.[26]

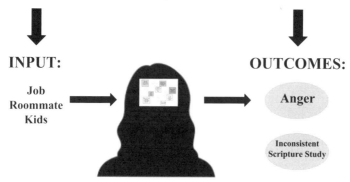

Change most often happens when we focus on what is in the center of this diagram: the things that are going on inside. Sister Wendy Watson Nelson even taught, "Through my research with families, I have come to believe that therapeutic change occurs as the belief that is at the heart of the matter is identified, challenged, or solidified." She then added: "What beliefs about yourself, others, or life constrain you from taking the next step toward making the changes you desire in your life?"[27]

Hence, a father can make a hundred different goals to not get angry with or yell at his kids, but if he doesn't ever change the beliefs and expectations he has about them, he will probably continue to get angry with them. We can try to change our circumstances all day long, but they will still filter through the exact same beliefs, expectations, and definitions that are still there. And if those beliefs, expectations, or definitions are false or unrealistic or incorrect in any way, they will produce negative emotions and behavior.

Instead, we can ask ourselves, "What is it I believe about this person or situation that causes me to be impatient or frustrated or angry?" "Why do I hate my job?" "What do I *truly* believe about scripture study?"

If, in this process, I discover that I really don't believe scripture study makes any difference in my life, I am probably not going to become consistent at reading my scriptures, no matter what changes I might make in my schedule or my behavior. Yet, as I work on changing that belief — really focusing my prayers and faith on what is promised when we study our scriptures, for instance — my scripture study habits can begin to change.

_____

_____

_____

_____

_____

_____

_____

_____

_____

[1] The names have been changed in this story

[2] Elder Russell M. Nelson, "The Atonement," *Ensign*, November 1996; Atonement is Middle English for "at one with" or in harmony with

[3] Isaiah 61:3

[4] Sister Joy D. Jones, "Let me point out the need to differentiate between two critical words: *worth* and *worthiness*. They are not the same. Spiritual *worth* means to value ourselves the way Heavenly Father values us, not as the world values us. Our worth was determined before we ever came to this earth. 'God's love is infinite and it will endure forever.' (D. Todd Christofferson, "Abide in My Love," *Ensign*, November 2016, 48) On the other hand, *worthiness* is achieved through obedience. If we sin, we are less worthy, but we are never worth less! We continue to repent and strive to be like Jesus with our worth intact." ("Value Beyond Measure," *Ensign*, November 2017)

[5] The concept of belief boxes, belief windows, or even just the power our beliefs have in our lives has been shared and developed in many different formats. Stephen R. Covey established a clear, relatable concept when he taught about paradigms in *The 7 Habits of Highly Effective People.* (1999). London: Simon & Schuster. pp. 30-31. Virginia H. Pearce added additional perspective to this idea in her book *Through His Eyes: Rethinking What You Believe About Yourself.* (2011). Salt Lake City, UT: Deseret Book. Sister Wendy Watson Nelson taught about the power of beliefs in her talk "Change: It's Always a Possibility," BYU Devotional, April 7, 1998. The concepts and diagrams created for this chapter are a combination of all these ideas.

[6] President Thomas S. Monson has stated, "We are the product of all we read, all we view, all we hear and all we think." (*Teachings of Thomas S. Monson,* comp. Lynne F. Cannegieter (2011), 267.) We might also find here some of the spiritual knowledge we came to earth with, possibly from the lessons we were taught by the Father in the world of spirits before we were ever born (see D&C 138:56). These could be things we "just seem to have always known" or truths that are immediately familiar when we learn them for the first time.

[7] This process is a little more complicated than illustrated. Some of the factors involved with an idea becoming a belief include repetition, extreme circumstances, and the influence of the Spirit. We also tend to believe more readily something taught by someone we love or highly respect, even if it's somewhat ridiculous. Our emotions and mental vulnerability also play a part.

[8] Elder Boyd K. Packer, "Little Children," *Ensign*, November 1986; Beliefs can also be expectations, assumptions, definitions, opinions, and other ideas in there, as well. Each of these things represent how we see the world, what we expect of others, what we assume will happen, and how we define different aspects of life. For our purposes here, we will clump them together and call them beliefs.

[9] Stephen R. Covey explained, "Between stimulus and response there is a space. In that space lies our freedom and power to choose our response." (*7 Habits*) It seems our beliefs could be found somewhere in that space between stimulus and response.

[10] "Little Children," *Ensign*, November 1986

[11] "Lift Where You Stand," *Ensign*, November 2008, emphasis added

[12] Elder Richard G. Scott taught, "The inspiring influence of the Holy Spirit can be overcome or masked by strong emotions, such as anger, hate, passion, fear, or pride.

When such influences are present, it is like trying to savor the delicate flavor of a grape while eating a jalapeño pepper. Both flavors are present, but one completely overpowers the other. In like manner, strong emotions overcome the delicate promptings of the Holy Spirit." ("To Acquire Spiritual Guidance," *Ensign*, November 2009)

[13] Some scholars believe that Tarshish was geographically probably one of the farthest places Jonah could realistically go from Nineveh at that time.

[14] I understand that forgiveness can be a complicated thing. I do not, in any way, want to minimize the process it takes to forgive others who have wronged us, especially when it is something severe. The only point I am making from this is that receiving an impression from the Lord to forgive someone can cause negative feelings in us that in many ways are not because the revelation is wrong, or that it was wrong for God to ask it of us, but because what we might believe about that other person or our responsibility is.

[15] Isaiah 1:18

[16] "Come, Join with Us," *Ensign*, November 2013

[17] Moses 3:17; 4:6-11

[18] Chapter 2: God the Eternal Father," *Teachings of Presidents of the Church: Joseph Smith* (2011), 36–44

[19] Matthew 22:36-40

[20] You may have heard the legend about an old man who had two wolves fighting each other within him. One wolf represented anger, guilt, superiority, and lies; the other embodied peace, faith, compassion, and humility. And the fate of their survival depended on one thing: which one of them was fed. Like these wolves, both truths and untruths must be fed to survive. Truth needs to be nurtured and strengthened. Lies must be continually reinforced. We may not be consciously aware of it, but we expend effort to keep either of them alive.

[21] "Little Children," *Ensign,* November 1986

[22] "If Ye Had Known Me," *Ensign*, November 2016, emphasis added

[23] For some great insights on this concept of labeling and acknowledging our beliefs, I recommend the book *The Happiness Trap* by Russ Harris (Trumpeter Publishing, 2014). It goes into more detail some ways we can take control of our thoughts.

[24] Elder David A. Bednar, "In The Strength of the Lord," *Ensign*, November 2004

[25] "Born of God," *Ensign*, July 1989

[26] "Little Children," *Ensign,* November 1986

[27] "Change: It's Always a Possibility!" BYU Devotional, April 7, 1998; Also found in *Beliefs: The Heart of Healing in Families and Illness,* Lorraine M. Wright, Wendy L. Watson, and Janice M. Bell. (1996). New York: Basic Books

HINDRANCE #4

Casting Our Eyes About

In Lehi's magnificent dream, a tree bearing brilliant white fruit stood in the middle of an open field. There was a path with a rod of iron running alongside it leading to this glorious tree, which Lehi later learned represented the Savior. And Lehi could see multitudes of people trying to make their way to it (see 1 Nephi 8).

But the way to this tree was not free from distractions. There was a large building full of finely dressed yet loudly mocking people in the distance, a filthy river raging nearby, strange roads leading to unknown destinations, and a mist of darkness that hung thick and heavy around the path.[1] It is no wonder, then, that although many seemed to want to, very few actually reached the tree. Instead, they were drawn away from the path by those in the building, the strange roads, or the darkness.

We then learn of two groups of people who got onto the path, held to the rod, and made their way past all those obstacles to the tree. However, as the first group ate the fruit of the tree, they immediately did something interesting: "They did cast their eyes about . . ." (1 Nephi 8:25). Here they were standing in front of a tree that was whiter and more precious and more beautiful than anything Lehi had ever seen. It offered a fruit that was "most desirable above all things" (11:22). Indeed, they were standing at the feet of the Savior and, instead of worshipping Him, they started looking around them. Lehi explains that they even seemed "ashamed." And so, they left the tree and "fell away into forbidden paths and were lost" (v. 28).

However, as the second group passed through those same circumstances to get to the tree, they did something in stark contrast to those in the preceding verses: "They came forth and fell down and partook of the fruit of the tree" and "heeded . . . not" all of the things that were going on around them (vs. 30, 33).

What was it that made these two groups different from each other? It wasn't whether they stayed on the path. It wasn't whether they held onto the iron rod as they pressed forward through the darkness, which we later learn was a symbol for the word of God. It wasn't even whether they partook of the fruit of the tree which represented the love of God as manifested in the gift of His Son.

The difference was, at least in part, *where* they chose to look as they stood at the foot of that tree; for where they chose to look — for approval, help, whatever it was — seemed to determine, in the end, what they did.

As a miraculous account for our day, these ten short verses in the Book of Mormon reveal one of the great challenges of our day: where are we going to look? God stands ready to help us. He is pouring down divine instruction, knowledge, and approval from heaven. The world, however, is also throwing instruction, knowledge, and approval our way. Now more than ever before, its loud, incessant voices want to tell us who we are, what we should be doing, and what is important in this life.

We have to decide which direction we are going to look (or at least evaluate where we are *already* looking), for that focus will end up determining what we do.

When it came down to it, that first group seen by Lehi did not have their focus, nor it seems their faith, permanently fixed on the tree. Maybe the building was where their hearts were turned all along. Maybe they were clinging to the rod of iron so tightly because they were afraid they might let go.[2] Or maybe it was a complete surprise to them that, in that moment of decision, they not only looked to the building, but also forsook what Christ was offering them. We don't really know.

However, we have to know where *we* are looking and why. Are we looking around horizontally for approval? Do we trust the world's solutions or advice more than God's? Do we *think* our eyes and hearts and minds are fixed vertically on God but, in truth, they aren't?

Anytime we cast our eyes horizontally to the guidance, solutions, or approval the world is offering, we weaken the flow of heaven's guidance, solutions, and approval in our lives. Indeed, this is another way we hinder revelation in our lives.

Let me show you what this competition between the horizontal and the vertical in our lives can look like:

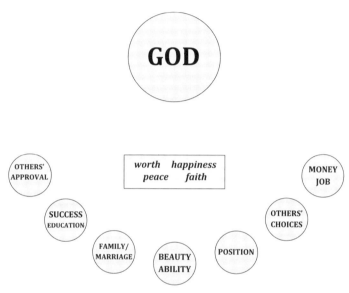

In this diagram, there is a box in the middle that represents some of the things that we seek in this life to define and enrich our identity and purpose — things like worth, happiness, peace, and faith. Certainly, many other things could be listed in this box such as hope, acceptance, love, fulfillment, trust, respect, confidence, peace, or validation. However, for the purpose of the diagram, I've just listed a few. They are all incredibly interconnected.[3]

The bottom half of this diagram has circles representing different external facets of our mortal experience — things such as what others think of us, what degree we obtained, our athleticism, how much money we make, our marital status, how good of a family we have, etc. Some of these things are within our control, some of them are not. Either way, we could call this the "horizontal" in our lives.

You can also see that God is in the top circle. He, and all the divine and eternal things that emanate from Him, could be called the "vertical" in our lives.

Because of the divine gift of agency, we can largely choose how to fulfill those needs in the middle box, for we can choose where we are going to look to fulfill those needs. Whatever we choose to look to, we make, in a sense, a connection to, with some connections being stronger than others. It could be illustrated like this:

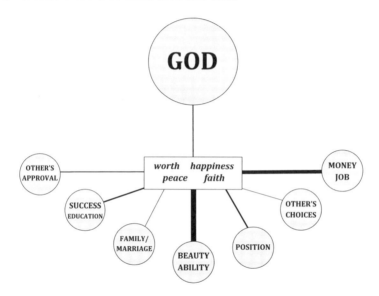

This particular diagram could represent someone who relies heavily on his physical appearance or abilities for his worth and who ties much of his happiness to how much money he makes. Maybe he also puts a lot of emphasis on the fact that he's earned a Master's degree and is the boss of his company. Notice that because of the strength of his connection to those horizontal things, his connection to God is, by default, more thin and weak.

These horizontal connections, as well as the strength of these connections, will look different for each one of us simply because different things matter to different people. Yet, this competition between the horizontal and the vertical applies to all of us.

Let me quickly share some real-life examples.

One young woman shared with me: "I have always been very smart and quite good at math. Everything came super easy to me. I came to college and took a math class and did horrible in it. All of a sudden, I began questioning everything about myself. I had always been the smart girl and so I became unsure of who I was for a while."

Another young man confided: "I've watched my father struggle with just about every relationship he has. I finally realized one day why: he connects his worth to his opinion. If you don't agree with his opinion, he thinks you don't like him, causing him to argue, get offended, and be on the defense in most situations. It is sad to me because most of us kids don't like talking to him, but it's not because we don't like him. We just don't like the conflict."

Some of us connect our worth to something that is a product of our creativity, ability, or interests. For example, a mother can take the criticism of a dinner very personally because her worth is tied to her homemaking abilities. Or a father might stubbornly insist on an inflated selling price for a home he dedicated a lot of time and energy building for his family. When we make these connections, creating something beautiful can be rewarding, but if it turns out to be a disaster it can also be very discouraging; the praise of others can be gratifying but their criticism or rejection can be crushing.

What if we connect our happiness or identity to our job? What could be the consequence of that? We might choose work over family, or struggle when we have to quit that job to start a family. We might compromise our standards just to keep a job. Or we might begin to believe that our worth increases as our success in a job increases. Connecting our worth in this way causes us to feel differently about *ourselves* as a person, not just our *ability* in a job, and I believe it could partly be why the loss of a job is so devastating.

We can also connect the fulfillment of our needs to something that happens in someone else's life: i.e., happiness that is dependent on my daughter winning student body president or acceptance from others because of my family's wealth. Maybe we even determine our value or worthiness to be loved based on our ability to make other's happy. However, making that horizontal connection must also mean that my parent's bankruptcy changes my standing with others or that if one of my children loses an election, fails a math class, or even gets caught stealing, then I'm no good and I can't be happy. It must mean that if I cannot make other's "happy" all of the time (whatever *that* really means), I am pathetic. Again, it is almost impossible not to feel some kind of failure or other destructive emotion from something negative that happens in someone else's life if we also connect our value as a person to something positive in someone else's life.

Lastly, we can even make horizontal connections with spiritual things. A friend of mine was once talking with a man he didn't know very well. They were traveling together for an assignment, and in the first hour alone the man repeatedly mentioned his time as bishop of his ward. He had recently been released, and so my friend thought to himself, "Well, he's fresh out of the experience, and so it just must be on his mind." However, as they continued their journey, the topic came up again and again.

My friend only shared this story with me because of what he had been taught from that experience: it compelled him to ask himself, "How many times have I done the same thing in one way or another?" We can attach our identity to our calling, our worth to how well we teach Sunday School, or our worthiness to how easy it is for us to be a Cubmaster. And these connections seem to become even more evident to us when these righteous endeav rs "fail" in some way.

These are just a few examples. What is interesting to point out, however, is that no matter where we turn, no matter what direction we are looking, we will find some version of what we are looking for. However, just like those in Lehi's dream, when we are looking horizontally for approval or happiness or worth or anything else, we can't also be looking vertically to God for those things. We cannot, in this sense, look to "both God and mammon" (Luke 16:13). Indeed, we hinder heaven's influence in our lives if we have strong connections to the horizontal worldly influences around us.

Think about this: How can we be divinely guided if we constantly seek answers from worldly sources? How can we find assurance from our Father in Heaven if we look to our bank account for security? How can we be filled with eternal joy if we keep allowing our happiness to be based on our accomplishments? How can we hear God's approval about our parenting if we gauge our success by our children's choices? Or how will we truly lean upon the arm of the Lord if we insist upon carrying our burdens ourselves?

The scriptures teach that when our "hearts are set so much upon the things of this world," whatever worldly things they are, "the heavens withdraw themselves" (D&C 121:35-36). But I've also wondered if when our hearts are seeking out the things of the world, *we* withdraw ourselves from the heavens.[4]

It seems this might be what this rebuke to David Whitmer was referring to. The Lord said: "Behold . . . you have feared man and have not relied on me for strength as you ought. But your mind has been on the things of the earth more than on the things of me, your Maker . . . and you have not given heed unto my Spirit. . . . Wherefore, you are left to inquire for yourself" (D&C 30:1-3). It seems Brother Whitmer was giving heed to a lot of horizontal things around him, but not necessarily to the Spirit. In what ways might we be "left to ourselves" when our minds are more focused on the things of the earth?

In many ways, it also seems when we cast our eyes about to the people or circumstances around us, we hand over power in our lives to those people or circumstances. We allow those things to tell us who we are, what our purpose is, what is important, and even what choices to make.

I found the insight from this young mother so intriguing: "I really had no idea I thought this, but I've realized that what others think of me is really what I think of me. My confidence in myself is almost completely based on the confidence others have in me. How I see myself is so tightly connected to how other people see me that it is very hard for me to see anything else. In fact, if others are upset with me for any reason, I am immediately convinced that *I* must be wrong, and usually start feeling horrible about myself. I've realized that sometimes I can't even hear what God is trying to tell me over what I am listening to from my husband, children, friends, neighbors, or even total strangers. And that connection is influencing not just how I feel, but what I say and the choices I make."

How can we possibly hear what the Lord is telling us if other's voices are what we are really listening for? Even if those voices come from trusted people in our lives, they are still not the Lord's voice. I say that carefully because I know we need each other and I know we must rely on each other for feedback or guidance. The only problem is that a young, overwhelmed, exhausted mother may have a very difficult time giving herself permission to question whether those voices are always relevant to her and her situation. But she must question it — not to find an excuse not to listen to others, but simply to make sure that what she is listening to is really what is best for her, or better yet what the Lord thinks.

I had a young man share with me that shortly after he got home from his mission, he got invited to go to a movie with some friends. The transition back into a social life is sometimes rough for a returned missionary, and so he said the invitation was so welcome. However, something in the back of his mind told him that maybe he should check out the movie beforehand. Almost as quickly as that thought came into his mind, he said another thought stopped him: "If I find the movie inappropriate, they will think I'm just an overzealous returned missionary, and they won't invite me again." So, he just decided to go.

That night during the movie, he discovered that, indeed, it was probably something he shouldn't be watching. But, he said, again the thought came: "I can't leave. They will think I'm such a fool. Besides, most of these guys are returned missionaries, too." And so he stayed.

The first group to the Tree of Life may have been obedient and faithful followers of Jesus Christ, but their horizontal connection to the approval of those in the building was what, in the end, influenced their choices. *The horizontal must have mattered more to them.* So, they not only looked over to the building for approval, they ended up abandoning everything they had just done to join them. It seems we should ever underestimate the pull of the building. If we keep our focus on it long enough, it is going to pull us down and pull us away from the things that will ultimately bless us and save us. Our connection to other's choices or approval can override good intentions and even deeply held values, causing us to be at the mercy of our circumstances.[5] That connection can also often override the impressions the Spirit may be trying to give us.

In fact, I have always wondered if the rich young man was surprised or saddened as he walked away sorrowful from the obedience he had been committing to since he was young (Matthew 19:22). Could this be one reason why we can be doing what seem to be "all the right things" and still, like the rich young man, walk away from eternal things?

Sister Joy D. Jones gave this idea another perspective: "If the pull of the world is stronger than the faith and trust we have in the Savior, then the pull of the world will prevail every time."[6] Could this be why our trials sometimes drive us to distraction instead of sending us to our knees? Is it because our connection to something tangible but temporary is stronger than our connection to God?[7]

As hard as some of the truths in these questions may be, I find great hope in another truth: as our vertical connection to God becomes stronger, our connection to horizontal things will, by default, become weaker, looking something like this:

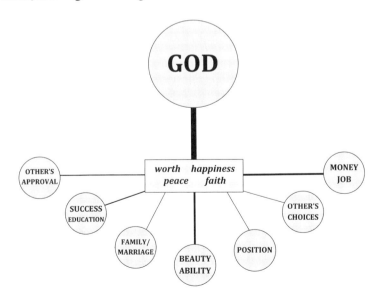

As our faith and trust in God become stronger than the pull of the world, His influence will prevail! We will find ourselves turning to Him in our experiences, grounding ourselves onto a foundation of truth, and opening up our lives for His guidance, reassurance, and love. We will, as Sister Rosemary M. Wixom explained, "take our validation vertically from Him, not horizontally from the world around us or from those on Facebook or Instagram."[8] When we do this, revelation can flow so much abundantly in our lives.

The process to disconnect these tethers to the temporal and temporary around you may look different for you than it does for me. It's a personal journey that requires some soul-searching and sincere prayer. However, it almost always involves letting God redefine some things in our hearts and minds.

I once heard about a couple who had accumulated, in the pursuit of a certain lifestyle, hundreds of thousands of dollars of debt. As they tried to unravel the mess, they had to move, sell almost everything they could, and give up so many of their familiar comforts. In that process, the husband explained, "This has been much more difficult than I thought — and not because I can't drive a nice car anymore. *I have had to completely rewire how I value myself* and how I determine the value of a person in general."

Yet, what a beneficial rewiring process it can be. We can ask the Lord to help us redefine and disconnect our *real* worth from our *net* worth, not only opening our eyes to the horizontal measuring stick we may have been using, but also, by default, weakening our connection to that measuring stick.[9] Slowly but surely, our vertical connection with heavenly definitions and heavenly reassurance can became more solid, and our connection to horizontal reassurance can be lessened.

This process may also require us to unravel our worldly webs and simplify our lives. It might involve making an effort to know God better than the familiar things we are relying on at the moment. Regardless of what we feel heaven beckoning us to do, we can disconnect from whatever horizontal thing in our life is dominating our lives, even if that connection looks like a multi-strand steel cable.

In this process, we come to know a Being who offers true confidence and lasting assurance that fills our deepest needs; we find in Him love, acceptance, and approval that can be all that we need, even if we don't always get those things from the people who matter most to us. In Him, we find exquisite joy and the deepest of fulfillment. We find real, lasting versions of faith, happiness, peace, success, and worth. And what we find from Him can completely override any temporal source in our lives.

Here's an inspiring story of one woman's journey of experiencing this power in her own life. Six months into her marriage, Jane's[10] husband came to her and told her that he was not physically attracted to her anymore. It wasn't that he didn't want to be married to her, he was just embarrassed to admit that she wasn't beautiful to him. Jane couldn't believe it. And over time she became more and more obsessed with that reality.

At first, she thought it was her fault. She thought that maybe something she did or didn't do would change how he felt about her. Then she began praying for a miracle to change his heart. Nothing seemed to change. And then she shared this:

> "A miracle did happen. But it had nothing to do with what my husband thought about me. During this time of deep pain and insecurity, I finally realized that I was looking in the mirror in my bedroom and the mirror in my husband's eyes instead of the mirror inside my heart.
>
> "At some point, I remembered there was another mirror, and I took a long look at myself. Deep down inside me, a voice reassured me that I was actually beautiful enough. The strength I had forgotten welled up in me, and I knew that what my husband thought about my attractiveness was not all that important. I could value him without taking on his weaknesses, including his inability to see my beauty.
>
> "Something changed in me that day. I wanted to keep that strength with me, and I knew I would have to choose to believe in my beauty, even if no one else did. I prayed to overcome self-defeating thoughts, to avoid hatred, anger, and

jealousy, which always bring self-doubt. I quit blaming my husband for his blindness and began being good to myself.

"That is my miracle. And although it doesn't change a thing, I just want to mention that last week, my husband began to cry. He apologized for how he felt about me at the beginning of our marriage. He says he has discovered that I really am beautiful. The problem was inside him. He can't believe he said those things to me. He says he thinks I am the most beautiful woman he knows. And I already knew that."[11]

What an amazing gift it is that we have this power; we can decide what has power in our lives. We get to decide where we are going to look.[12] We get to decide how our needs will be fulfilled. And, thus, we get to decide where our revelation is going to come from.

The more that we look vertically and disconnect from the horizontal in our lives, the more divine revelation will flow in our lives. The more we look to God, the more we will consistently and consciously put ourselves in the way of pure divine revelation from heaven instead of the often destructive, but almost always hollow "revelation" from the world.

Therefore, What?

As you think about where you are really looking for answers, hope, peace, happiness, validation, or faith in your life, consider a few things:

Examine your connections. One way to figure out where you are really looking is to begin to figure out what your own connections are. One time I was presenting this concept to a group of adults. A sister in the room later contacted me and shared that, as we were talking about what we connect our worth and happiness to, the Spirit inspired her to make a list of all the different connections she had made in her life. And so, she went home and began to think about what her worth was connected to, what her happiness was defined by, where she was looking for peace, what her faith was centered on, etc.

She said it took a long time to be able to identify and uncover where she was looking. Yet as she did, she realized something she had not known before: she was casting her eyes about far more than she realized. It was incredibly surprising to her.

Create a Connection Inventory. Consider making a similar list. Begin to define things in your life: "My worth is defined by . . ." "Happiness is found in . . ." "My faith is in . . ." You can do this with hope, peace, validation, confidence, or anything else you feel you need to define in your life. This list may have some similarities to your Belief Inventory because you are essentially trying to discover what you *believe* about these things. What is your worth really based on? Where are you truly seeking validation? Where do you honestly believe happiness is found? What are you placing your faith or trust in?

A few who have gone through this process shared things like this:

"I look to horizontal sources to fix my problems because I realized I don't really trust spiritual fixes."

"I pray sincerely about my challenges and then get up from my knees and stress and worry and fear."

"I realized I often turn to making more money to give me security."

"I try to solve problems that I now realize only God can solve."

You could also fill in your own Horizontal/Vertical diagram.

What needs would you put in the center box? What would your circles have in them? How thick of a line would you draw between them? How thick would your line up to God be?

83

In this process, you may discover ideas that you weren't aware of. You may understand better why you do what you do, feel what you feel, struggle with the things you struggle with, or even why revelation isn't working in your life the way you are expecting.

You might also discover more evidence that what you *know* and what you *believe* are two different things. If you know you are a child of God with divine worth and eternal potential, but the first thing you do in the morning is check to see what others have said about you on social media; or you rely on others' praise for a lesson, proposal, or parenting idea; or you avoid correction from someone because it will destroy your "self-esteem," it just might be that you don't actually *believe* yet what you *know* about divine worth.

What lens are we looking through? Another way we can discover what we are connecting our needs to is to identify the lens through which we are looking at our lives. One young woman I knew was really struggling because she never expected that she would be near graduation and not married. All she really wanted was to get married and have a family, and because that didn't seem to be happening in the near future, she was completely unsure about herself and what to do with her life.

As we were talking, I felt to pick up a pair of my glasses and say, "Rachel, let's say these glasses represent marriage and motherhood. You are looking at your life through these glasses. As long as you define yourself by whether or not you are married or have children, you will struggle with how you see yourself and will not be able to see things clearly."

I then picked up a different pair of glasses. "These," I said, "are the glasses of discipleship. If you look at your life through these glasses, what do you see?"

"I guess I see someone who is striving to be worthy," she said, "someone who has made a lot of progress and has learned a lot these last few years."

"OK, good," I said. "Now you can see more clearly. Marriage and motherhood are eternal and good, but they cannot be the only lens through which you look to see yourself or to determine your worth. God doesn't love us more when we are married. We are not of more worth to Him if we have children. He doesn't see us through those lenses. He sees us as one of His children, as a disciple of His Son. And when we put those glasses on, we see ourselves as He sees us."

Sometimes, we can become confused about what indicates not only that we matter, but that we matter to God. We might forget that God doesn't seem to look at us through the lens of our circumstances — if that be married or divorced, rich or poor, handsome or homely, successful or struggling.

It also seems He does not bless every one of us with the same specific opportunities as an indication of His love or validation. He does not connect our worth to whether or not we are a mother, nor to how successful our efforts have been to raise up righteous children. He does not connect our worth to whether or not we are a Stake President, nor to how successful we are at our job.

What does God think? One way to stop our horizontal thinking dead in its tracks is to begin asking questions like this: "What does God think about this?" "What does He know?" "How does God feel about me even though this happened?" As we consciously seek to know how God feels about something, it re-routes this connection, regardless of where it was. When we begin to ask questions like these, it invites *His* revelation. In fact, I have found that *questions in general invite revelation*. We are asking for the Lord to *teach* us instead of *telling* Him what we think we already know.

When we seek to know how He feels we are fulfilling our role as a spouse or how He feels about our performance at work, it weakens the power the world has over us in defining those roles. When we seek to know how He feels about the foreclosure of our home or about our son being in jail, we become more able to set aside what others may think about them. We must come to know how *He* really sees us and our circumstances.

One sister shared this profound insight with me recently that is a perfect example of understanding this kind of truth: "I have realized that God doesn't love me because *I'm* perfect. He loves me because *He's* perfect." Turning our hearts and souls to God and His divine and perfect criteria, we weaken the horizontal because we are strengthening the vertical in our lives.

Where is our "revelation" really coming from? This process of distinguishing where our impressions, or the interpretations of those impressions, is coming from can be so beneficial. However, realize that we can, in a sense, receive "revelation" (or guidance, inspiration, motivation) from *any* horizontal source — not just the world or Satan, but also our anger, our fear, our guilt, our circumstances, even our hormones or our pain.

Years ago, Michelle had an interesting experience with receiving "revelation" from a source neither of us had considered. She was asked to fill an important position at our children's school. Initially, she felt really good about it. She had a lot of great ideas about how she would run the program, and all the ways she could make it better. She was really excited about it, and almost accepted it immediately, but decided to give it some more thought.

She shares: "After about a week, I started realizing some of the ramifications of the decision. It would require a significant amount of time away from my family, and on nights when my husband would not be able to be home with our younger children. It would require me to be gone right after school when my other children would be coming home. The more I thought about it, the more I could see how hard it would be on all of us if I accepted the position. It got to the point that every time I thought about it, I would get sick to my stomach. I realized I shouldn't accept it, but it was a very hard thing to turn down. Although I was so excited about it and felt so good about it at first, I later realized that my feelings were not necessarily inspired by *God* but rather by *flattery*. I felt honored that I was being considered and I interpreted those feelings to be an affirmation from the Spirit."

Finding hope and healing from mental struggles. Another interesting but unexpected benefit from evaluating our connections is that it often exposes at least one possible reason we could be struggling with depression, anxiety, or some other emotional or mental struggle. And these issues can so often get in the way of revelation.

Not knowing where we stand before God compels us to seek validation from something, anything — whether that be others' approval, success, wealth, or any number of tangible or immediate things around us. And if how we feel about ourselves is so closely tied to something worldly that is unstable or out of our control, then how we feel about ourselves will constantly be at the mercy of something unstable or out of our control! If our worth is tied to something external like other people's agency, then our worth will be at the mercy of their agency. Our perception of our lives, or how happy or peaceful or faithful we are, will be constantly fluctuating with our changing circumstances — almost like a roller coaster.

It seems, then, that of course we will feel anxious! Of course we will feel often feel down! Indeed, I believe there are very few other emotions we will feel *but* uneasiness or unhappiness or hopelessness when we connect our worth to something external that is out of our control or something temporal that will ultimately fail us.

One woman shared how this process has personally benefitted her: "This one aspect of learning about where I am really looking for happiness or worth, combined with what I now know about false beliefs, has probably had the most impact on my life. After struggling for years with depression, the Lord slowly helped me see that, although there were also some physical issues going on, underlying most of it were completely false, unrealistic, and unhealthy beliefs about myself and my life. I believed the Lord judged my worth on what I accomplished and how successful I was. I believed His definition of a good mother was one who could do everything perfectly. Happiness, in my mind, was found in getting my way. Peace could only be found in having no trials.

"And so, I worked my way into a debilitating depression because I couldn't accomplish what I believed the Lord expected me to accomplish. I wasn't living to the level of perfection I believed He expected me to live. I couldn't meet those expectations. I was also feeling defeated and sometimes in total despair because I was failing at what mattered most to me, which was pleasing Him by fulfilling the divine role He had asked me to fulfill."

If you, or someone you know and love, is struggling with any of these mental challenges, I suggest taking stock of what you are really connecting your happiness or worth to. As you begin to unravel these thoughts in your head, you will not only find a freedom from some of the absolutely unattainable connections you have made, but also a freedom to truly follow the Lord's will in your life as He reveals it to you.

Actually redirect your horizontal connections to something eternal. Lastly, as you strive to disconnect your life from the horizontal around you, seek diligently to actually reconnect each aspect of it to a divine source. Let me explain:

Recently, Michelle and I were having a conversation about a weakness of hers — a tendency she has to connect a part of her worth to something horizontal. She couldn't figure out why, after years of tackling it, that horizontal connection kept showing up and causing her so much stress. Even though she felt she was making progress in it, the same struggles would reappear again and again. As we were talking, I felt to ask her this question: "So, in your efforts to disconnect your worth from this temporal aspect of your life, what have you connected it to instead? Have you actually connected it vertically?"

That question opened up a huge realization: she may have been working very hard to make that disconnection, but hadn't actually reconnected her worth back to God and how He felt about her. One reason she knew this was because she couldn't really explain how God felt about her in that way; she didn't really know the eternal truths she should be relying on and trusting in instead. And so, by default, that need to feel of worth kept sliding back down to something horizontal.

When we find the wisdom or strength to begin disconnecting our worth, for example, from our success at work, we may, if we are not careful, just reconnect it to some other temporal success — like running a marathon or obtaining another degree or even fulfilling our calling — instead of connecting it to God and His definition of success.

Elder Paul E. Koelliker counseled that we have to both "remove the distractions that pull us toward the world *and* exercise our agency to seek Him," a combination I believe is essential to really be able to overcome this worldly influence in our lives.[13] When we do, Elder Koelliker promised that "we open our hearts to a celestial force which draws us toward Him," a "gravitational pull from heaven," that I have found is so much stronger than the pull of the horizontal around us.[14]

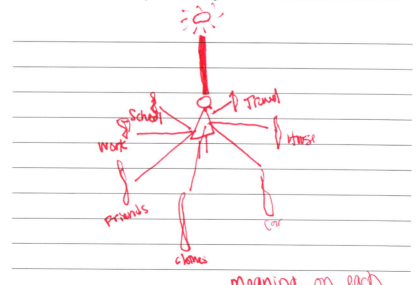

False Belief Villains

Superhero
of
TRUTH

---

[1] 1 Nephi 8

[2] 1 Nephi 8:24

[3] Our happiness is connected to our worth. Our peace is connected to our faith. Our faith is connected to our worth. However, it seems that our *worth* influences each of them. At the core of our ability to find happiness, feel hope, experience peace, find fulfillment, feel successful, feel worthy of acceptance, and even other things like exercising faith or being obedient *is what we believe our value is to ourselves, others, the world in general, and even God.* To feel of worth seems to be an innate, fundamental need. Why? I'm not completely sure. But I have wondered if it is an eternal, spiritual need that has to do with our separation from God and our eternal purpose to seek out and find Him.

[4] Mosiah 2:36

[5] Elder Richard G. Scott taught, "The guiding principle in the pattern of decisions based upon circumstance is to make choices according to the outcome desired rather than upon what is right or wrong. There is no use of an underlying set of standards to consistently guide those decisions. Each choice is made upon what appears to give the most desired result now. One who follow this path is left to his own strength and capacity and the support of others who can be influenced to acct in his favor. Satan encourages choices to be made in this manner. It gives him the greatest opportunity to tempt an individual to make decisions that will be harmful even though they appear most appealing when made." ("The Power of Righteousness," *Ensign,* November 1998)

[6] "Value Beyond Measure," *Ensign,* November, 2017

[7] Sister Neill F. Marriott, "Abiding in God and Repairing the Breach, *Ensign,* November 2017

[8] "Discovering the Divinity Within," *Ensign,* November 2015; emphasis added

[9] Sister Joy D. Jones: "As President Brigham Young taught: 'The least, the most inferior spirit now upon the earth ... is worth worlds.' No matter what, we always have worth in the eyes of our Heavenly Father." ("Value Beyond Measure," *Ensign,* November 2017)

[10] A name was assigned to the young woman in this story for retelling purposes

[11] *Why I Don't Hide My Freckles Anymore: Perspectives on True Beauty*, Lisa Tensmeyer Hansen, LaNae Valentine (2013). Salt Lake City: Deseret Book; Sister Rosemary M. Wixom taught, "Our divine nature has nothing to do with our personal accomplishments, the status we achieve, the number of marathons we run, or our popularity and self-esteem." (Discovering the Divinity Within," *Ensign,* November 2015)

[12] We decide whether we are going to serve or get on Facebook when we are feeling lonely. We decide if we will pray or go shopping when we are feeling lost. We decide to watch a conference talk or watch Netflix when we are struggling. We decide if we will invest in relationships at home or spend more time at the office, volunteering, or in the gym when we are feeling worthless.

[13] Elder Paul E. Koelliker, "He Truly Loves Us," *Ensign,* May 2012; emphasis added

[14] "He Truly Loves Us," *Ensign,* May 2012

HINDRANCE #5

Wanting Specifics

Years ago, Michelle shared the following experience with me:

"Throughout my life, I have had many experiences where I have gone to the Lord seeking an answer through a priesthood blessing. It might have been because I was struggling emotionally with something. Or I was trying to make a decision about something important at the moment. Maybe it was the dozens of times I was searching for insight about how to navigate the wonderful world of raising teenagers or desperately trying to understand why I still hadn't changed something in me I really wanted to change.

"Whatever it was, usually when I would finally ask for a blessing, I was at my wit's end. I truly wanted and needed some specific answers.

"I found, however, that so many times instead of giving me the specific answers I needed or telling me what I should do in a confusing situation, the Lord would often give me what seemed to be vague counsel about the issue or guidance that felt irrelevant to my challenge. It seemed that sometimes He would not even address the issue at all.

"One time in particular, I was seeking to know how to discipline a certain child. I knew we needed to do something about his repeated negative behavior, but I had already tried so many things that hadn't worked. I just really needed some divine instruction that was going to work. In a blessing, the Lord counseled me, 'Just listen to him.' And that was it. He said nothing about the actual problem or what I was supposed to do about it.

"At the time, it was so frustrating to me. It just seemed like the Lord didn't care about me or about my success as a parent. I also wondered if maybe I just didn't deserve the answers I was looking for. This experience, and others like it, made me wonder if God just wanted me to flounder on my own without the help I needed. I actually even started struggling with my faith in priesthood blessings."

Does any of this thought process sound familiar? It seems one of our great struggles with revelation is about receiving *answers*. I've heard so many concerns in this regard:

- My college students, who are usually faced with a lot of big life decisions will often say, "Why isn't the Lord answering me?"
- Some youth struggle that their patriarchal blessing didn't give them more specific information than it did.
- A friend faced with an unusual illness that lasted for years faithfully prayed every day for some answers as to what is wrong with her, but still couldn't figure out what was wrong.
- One father expressed, "I wish He would just tell me if I've supposed to take this job."
- I recently had a conversation with an amazing sister named Laura who was feeling as if the Lord was simply not responding to her many years of pleading for answers about her financial struggles, almost as if He was ignoring her.
- I even heard one of our children once say, "Why should I pray about it? He's not going to tell me what to do anyway."

Indeed, we are definitely seeking answers, we just don't always feel like we are always getting them.

What I have found, however, is that often the Lord *is* answering us. I know that sometimes answers are slow in coming or don't seem to be coming at all. Sometimes, the heavens are silent for a period of time by "divine design," because there are lessons that need to be learned or experiences we need to have.[1] However, often the Lord is actually answering. We just might not be hearing the answer because we don't fully understand what to expect from the experience or we aren't aware of all the different ways God responds to man's petitions.

In other words, we can hinder revelation in our lives by wanting the Lord to give us a specific answer when it's not the kind of answer He's offering. Whenever we are looking for very specific counsel from the Lord for the struggle we are having in the moment, the only thing we're listening for is *a very specific answer*, all the while missing or disregarding any other form of guidance or direction He may be giving us.

For example, Laura eventually realized that the heavens hadn't been silent at all in her financial struggles. She had been receiving assurance in her moments of doubt, many witnesses of His love, unexplainable moments of peace, and even some thoughts and suggestions along the way about what to do financially.[2] She *had* been receiving answers, *she just hadn't received the solution to her problem*, and so she felt she hadn't received *anything*. Our Heavenly Father was teaching her, expanding her understanding, and, she later learned, preparing her (and others) for the solution.

That seems to have been the same challenge my wife was facing while seeking the Lord's help through priesthood blessings. Because God wasn't answering the concern she approached Him with, she didn't feel like He was answering at all.

Now, the Lord does sometimes give specifics. In fact, specific prayers often lead to specific answers. Nephi asked where to find ore to build a ship and God told him where to find it. Joshua was given very specific instructions that involved priests blowing trumpets and marching on a certain day and walking around Jericho a certain number of times in order to conquer that city. The young Joseph Smith asked which church was true and he was given a gloriously specific answer. Even consider again the Jaredites' experience. The Brother of Jared asked: How will we breathe? How will we see inside the boats? How will we steer? And God answered the Brother of Jared specifically what to do about the air. I'm sure some of us have had our own experience where God gave us a specific answer to a specific prayer, as well.

However, the truth is: God answers our specific concerns and questions in many different ways — not just with specific answers. After all, He told the Brother of Jared to solve the light issue himself, and He didn't even answer about how they should steer the barges.[3] Sometimes the answer is that we are supposed to decide ourselves if we want to take a different job. Sometimes the answer is that we just need to trust Him — and His divine timing and solutions — with our medical issues and He will take care of it. Both ways have divine reasoning and purpose. He is counseling and directing us in ways that are still answers, they just might not be in the form we are expecting.

What about the statement: "Why pray? He isn't going to tell me anyway?" I've wondered if one reason we might expect specifics is that, when we ask God a specific question, we assume we will automatically get a specific answer in return. That seems logical, right?

Think about the way we teach young children about prayer: if you pray, God will answer. Simple as that. Yet, while that is an absolutely true principle, I have learned that this process of asking and answering matures and expands as we spiritually mature and our understanding expands. God's method of answering takes on many different forms as we move through life and experience.[4] And because sometimes they take a new shape, these answers might be a little bit unfamiliar to us.

Thus, even just re-evaluating our definition of what an "answer" can look like helps us to see God's hand in our lives more clearly. And then we can answer the question of "Why pray?" with this reasoning: "Because He is going to hear me and He is going to give me exactly what I need in this moment, whatever that may be." The better we understand all the ways He helps His children, the better we become at discerning, receiving, and acting on revelation.

Part of this redefining I've done in my own life has been from discovering the role that *principles* play in our experience with revelation. We might not always recognize them as answers, yet I believe principles can be, when understood, one of the most valuable kind of answers we can receive. God sometimes doesn't give specifics because He is, instead, giving us *principles*.

I know we talk a lot about principles in the Church. They are interwoven into nearly every aspect of the gospel of Jesus Christ. However, I have discovered that many of us do not fully understand what they are. Not only that, we also often misunderstand the role they play in revelation. So, for the sake of understanding revelation better, let's back up a little bit so that we can understand principles a bit better.

When the Prophet Joseph Smith was asked, "How do you govern so great and diverse a people as the Latter-day Saints?" he answered, "I teach them correct principles and they govern themselves."[5] Elder Bruce R. McConkie responded to that teaching by saying, "That's the order of heaven. That's how the Almighty operates. That's how the Church is supposed to operate. We're supposed to learn correct principles and then govern ourselves."[6]

It seems that God uses eternal principles to govern His children so that His children can learn to govern themselves. And it seems He always has and He always will use principles for His purposes. He shares principles in the scriptures. He teaches principles through the words of living prophets.[7] A careful study of the parables the Savior taught in the New Testament also reveals they were vehicles for teaching underlying eternal principles. These truths gave guidance for man's behavior that was much more effective than a rule book or a checklist for daily living, like the law of Moses. And it is guidance that is still astonishingly applicable today!

Considering all of this, it would make sense, then, that in addition to the counsel He gives through His servants and His own ministry, the Lord would also reveal His will to us *through the Spirit* using principles.

In order to figure out what principles really are, we must first briefly talk about doctrines. Doctrines, Elder David A. Bednar explained, are fundamental teachings that provide answers to the *why* of the gospel.[8] For example, "The doctrine of the Atonement of Jesus Christ explains why Jesus Christ is our mediator and advocate with the Father."[9]

Principles, on the other hand, are *guidelines* that are based on doctrine. "Principles provide us with direction about the *what* and the *how*."[10] They are truths we live by, counsel we obey, and parameters that govern our attitudes and behavior that stem from doctrine.

Thus, what might we choose to *do* because we believe in the doctrine of the Atonement of Jesus Christ? Use the principle of repentance in our lives, exercise the principle of faith, show mercy, forgive others, etc. Principles can be concepts like obedience, humility, sacrifice, and patience, but they can also be guidelines like paying tithing, obeying the Word of Wisdom, and keeping the Sabbath day holy.

Next, a true principle will always have several key characteristics: it will be eternal, universal, and general.

Principles are unchanging. President Boyd K. Packer taught, "All the gospel principles that were true for Adam will still be true in the Millennium."[11] Principles are also true in all situations. Thus, they are not bound to age, gender, circumstance, background, personality, culture, geography, time, or any other changing facet of mortality. President Packer further explained, "Principles are not spelled out in detail. That leaves you free to find your way with an enduring truth, a principle, as your anchor."[12]

The principle of modesty, for example, fulfills all three of these criteria. Because it is unchanging, widely applicable, and not spelled out in detail, modesty can be lived by anyone, any age, living in any country, during any time in human history. In fact, it can not only apply to many different people and their different circumstances, but we can also use this same principle in our own lives many ways in many different situations.

Contrast that principle to a specific rule or standard, like wearing knee-length shorts. That directive doesn't fully represent the concept of modesty because it doesn't apply to everyone in every era in every situation in every country, does it? It's too specific. Sometimes specifics are necessary, but they are not the principle; they are, instead, based on the principle.

Elder Richard G. Scott also taught, "A true principle makes decisions clear even under the most confusing and compelling circumstances."[13] If we decide that we are going to live by the principle of modesty in all situations, our decisions can become very clear, even in compelling circumstances.[14] Like an anchor, it grounds us to truth while giving us enough freedom to make decisions and find our way in an ever-changing world.

Understanding what principles really are changes our obedience. It changes our faith and our discipleship. But it also changes our understanding of revelation. As Michelle began to identify these truths about principles herself, her experience with revelation completely changed. She shared:

"I was amazed as I started to understand what the Lord was trying to do. He wasn't giving me random counsel. He wasn't withholding the answers just to cause me to struggle. He was empowering me with eternal truths, with principles, instead of some temporary method or solution to the stress I was having in the moment. I wanted Him to tell me specifically what to do that day for the problem I was facing. But He was giving me a truth that could help me not only that day but in the many experiences I would have in the days and weeks and months ahead!

"It was also incredible to learn how that one small piece of what seemed like vague counsel the Lord gave us for our son — "listen to him" — was the very thing that was being neglected in our large and sometimes chaotic family. We learned over the years just how inspired those four words truly were for that son in particular, with his personality and his needs. It was something we came back to again and again, seeking the Spirit's direction of how and when we could do it better.

"In this process, I have learned that when God gives me principles, He is giving me a great gift. He is giving me the opportunity to figure out what the specifics of that principle will look like today and then, again, another opportunity to figure it out next week. He is also teaching me about Him, about how He feels about me, and about how He takes care of His children so that I can have faith in Him.

"That is, to me, one unexpected blessing of learning principles and learning how to live by them: you are naturally drawn to the doctrines they are based on. As I came to really understand what He was doing for me, I not only felt a deep love for my Heavenly Father for caring so much about me, but I sensed that He believed in me and in my ability to figure out how to use and apply that knowledge to bless my life."

We could liken our experience with principles and revelation to how a wise father would help his daughter with her math homework.

As he sits next to her, patiently guiding her through the process, it wouldn't do his daughter any good for him to take the paper from her at the first sign of struggle and fill in all the answers. Nor would it even do her any good for him to promptly tell her a specific answer when she doesn't know it.

If he gave her the answer to problem 12, she also wouldn't know how to do problems 17 and 19. Even if she is crying or throwing a fit or claiming the teacher didn't teach her how to do it, he knows he must guide her through learning how the math works so that she can learn to do it herself. She may not understand that in the moment and think her dad is just being mean, but *he* understands that.

Remember, our Heavenly Father seems most concerned about our eternal progression. He intricately and masterfully weaves so many lessons into our everyday experiences. As He teaches us, it feels like He, too, is often sitting right next to us as we work through our challenges, patiently guiding us through the process.

However, if He just gives us the answer to our own "problem 12" at the first sign of struggle, how many times does that help us? Once. Yet, if He teaches us the principle behind that problem, we will be able to apply that principle in challenges we will face later on. Even if we don't, *He* also knows we are not only going to eventually face those specific challenges, but many other problems that will require the understanding of that principle in the future! Our loving Father doesn't seem to just want to help us once. He commonly teaches us truths that will help us multiple times.

We talked at the beginning of this book about how sometimes revelation is difficult to receive simply because God's infinite ways are sometimes difficult for our finite minds to understand. He is teaching us about who He really is, something we are still trying to wrap our heads around. Principles seem to be one way we can know God would do in a situation because He lives by eternal principles to perfection. Thus, it seems God reveals principles to us to help us understand the perfections of His character that make Him a God. Our experiences with principles and revelation and having to prayerfully act on our own under the direction of the Spirit without Him spelling everything out for us seems to be preparing us for living a higher law, like He does.

Let's remember that it's not wrong to ask for specifics. The Lord will give very specific answers if that is what is needed in that moment. However, just knowing and understanding that there are many forms of "answers" that can be part of this process helps us to trust Him more and trust in the process more. It helps us to start looking for other manifestations of His ministering to us. It helps us realize that often there are greater objectives to be accomplished, greater rewards He desires to give us, and always greater purposes to be fulfilled.

It is also reassuring to know that regardless of how it feels, regardless of what answers we may or may not be getting, He *is* hearing us. He is listening even if we ask the wrong questions, even if we expect specific answers, even if we ask for what we shouldn't. He is hearing us. And He will continually and always teach us so that we will know not only how to ask for those answers but how to receive the answers He is willing to give.

These words given through the Prophet Joseph reaffirm that: "Verily I say unto you my friends, fear not, let your hearts be comforted; yea, rejoice evermore, and in everything give thanks;

"Waiting patiently on the Lord, for your prayers have entered into the ears of the Lord of Sabaoth, and are recorded with this seal and testament — the Lord hath sworn and decreed that they shall be granted.

"Therefore, he giveth this promise unto you, with an immutable covenant that they shall be fulfilled; and all things wherewith you have been afflicted shall work together for your good, and to my name's glory, saith the Lord" (D&C 98:1-3).

Therefore, What?

As we have talked about the role that principles play in our lives and specifically with revelation, are you recognizing times when the Lord gave you something besides a specific answer? Has He given you some truth that you might have disregarded because it wasn't what you wanted? Are there principles the Lord has been trying to teach you? Or do you feel more of a reassurance in your heart regarding an answer that just simply hadn't come yet?

Search for principles. I encourage you to pay attention to the principles the Lord has revealed to you as you've prayed for guidance, whether they came from an answer to prayer, priesthood blessings, or in unexpected impressions. As you continue to look for answers, seek out principles as you read your scriptures. Listen for principles in General Conference. The scriptures don't always have the specific answers we need for our circumstance, but I know they always have principles we can use in our circumstances.

If you are struggling to identify a principle in a situation, try putting it into an "if-then" statement. Nephi said, "I will go and do the things which the Lord hath commanded, for I know that the Lord giveth no commandment unto the children of men save He shall prepare a way for them to accomplish the thing which He hath commanded them."[15] One principle we could extract from that teaching is that *if* God commands me to do something, *then* He will provide a way for me to accomplish it. Clearly outlined like that, I can live by and trust in that principle over and over again throughout my life.

Use principles as anchors. President Packer compared principles to anchors. He taught that because principles are not spelled out in detail, they give us the freedom to figure things out and learn from our experiences while still having something to anchor us to truth. That analogy becomes even more meaningful when we learn how anchors function.

If a boat is sitting on top of eight feet of water, how long do you think the rope attached to its anchor needs to be? Ten feet? Maybe 15? That anchor actually needs *52 feet of rope*! In order for the boat to be able to adjust to the movement of the water, that rope needs to be at least five times the depth of the water. Also, the anchor itself actually needs to sit on its side for its fluke to dig into the sand on the bottom of the water, which requires extra length on the rope, as well.

If a boat is anchored over 10 feet of water with only 10 feet of rope and a three-foot swell comes along, then either the boat will be pulled under the water, or the anchor will break away from the boat. Stretched too tight, the anchor could also get dislodged from the bottom and the boat could get tossed out to sea.

When we use gospel principles like anchors attached to a 52-foot rope, they give us a lot of freedom to adjust to our changing circumstances. They give us something consistent to keep coming back to when we are parenting different children with completely different personalities, temperaments, and needs. Principles help us make media choices based on unchanging criteria, unlike the ever-changing standards of the world. Principles keep us anchored in safety.

Replace rules with principles. Lastly, one incredible blessing of learning about principles and how to live by them is that we begin to learn the difference between principles and rules. Some of us may be more comfortable with rules because they are set and predictable. They are a good place to start and can be used to establish clear boundaries, especially until more understanding and experience is gained.

However, when we learn the principles and doctrines behind a rule, commandment or standard, we are not bound by the "10-foot rope" of that rule. Rather, we are anchored with the freedom of the 52-foot rope. Like one young man realized: "Often I make a bunch of rules for every situation, keeping me tightly tethered to those rules, instead of finding the principle that can govern me in more than that situation." With principles, we become so much more free.

In fact, Elder Bednar taught, "We can reach a point where we are no longer are driven or directed by rules; instead, we learn to govern our lives by principle. To be sure, we keep the rules; but we also begin to ask ourselves, 'What is the principle involved here?' Such a person becomes less dependent upon external scaffolding and structure and more dependent upon quiet and ongoing divine direction."[16]

I find this truth so applicable as I teach young single adults about dating and marriage. Often, my students will wonder, "What are the rules to help us stay safe in the physical part of our relationship in terms of chastity?" In other words: "What *can* I do that is not going 'too far'?"

I often answer by telling them, "OK, so what you want me to do is give you a boundary that you have to stay in, right?" I then draw a big box on the board like this.

I explain that the box could represent the boundary of the commandment not to have sexual relations before marriage or outside of marriage. Thus, anything outside the box represents breaking that commandment.

"Now," I continue, "I'm going to give you some rules: Don't passionately kiss. Don't lie on top of each other. Don't go into each other's bedroom. And if you live by these rules, where are you living?" Inside that box, they usually say. I then draw a dotted line on the very inside edge of the box.

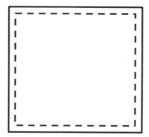

I then explain to them that when we live our lives this way, governed by a list of rules like this, we are usually living somewhere on that dotted line. This is not necessarily a bad thing; if we are staying within the boundary and being obedient, that is good.

But, think about this: when we live on that dotted line, is there a higher chance we will slip and cross the line of the standard? Maybe so. And what are the chances that we will not have a rule for every possible situation we find ourselves in? Possibly pretty high.

So, yes, rules may be a good place to start. However, instead of teaching a lot of rules, I try to help my students see the *doctrines* and *principles* behind the rules associated with dating. These doctrines and principles can protect them and guide them in *all* areas of dating, even unexpected and unforeseen situations, and not just with the physical side of their relationship but in all aspects.

We talk, for example, about the principle of chastity and its direct relation to the doctrine of the Atonement of Jesus Christ. I have my students discuss the doctrines regarding the sacred nature of the body and that these temples must not be defiled, for they were "bought with a price" (1 Corinthians 6:19-20).

From these doctrines, we find principles that can govern their behavior in dating such as service, bridling passions, and appropriate ways to express affection.

Then I erase the dotted line and draw a big circle in the middle of the box.

When doctrines and principles dictate and govern our behavior, they pull us away from the outer edge of the box and into a safer place somewhere in the middle.

Surprisingly, this area within the circle actually allows for a greater amount of freedom and is a much safer place to learn from our experiences, giving us a greater opportunity to hear and learn from the promptings of the Spirit as we go through our experiences. We are able, as Elder Bednar taught, to become "more dependent upon quiet and ongoing divine direction" than upon narrowly defined rules.

Using this model to teach truths about rules and principles is also incredibly helpful in parenting. In fact, it can be applied to any situation where the circumstances are constantly changing and we can't possibly come up with rules for everything that could happen in a given day.

So, the big question is: is it time to hang up a rule in your life and replace it with a principle? Is it time to figure out a principle for media choices in your family instead of a rule that can be incredibly frustrating every time we try to enforce it? And in what ways can we pull our focus to the center of that box, focusing on the Savior and His teachings?

If you do decide to start shifting from rules to principles in your family or other environments, understand that these kinds of wheels usually move slowly. It takes some adjustment, especially if rules are your favorite method for parenting or classroom management or decision making.

For instance, we stopped having a specific curfew rule for our teenagers and instead taught them some principles about self-control, responsibility, our physical and spiritual limitations as mortals when we are tired, preparing for the Sabbath day, and other facets that underlie the reason for a curfew. Each child has been given a different degree of leniency with the principle depending on their maturity, past responsibility, and desire to be obedient. As we have tried to live more by principle instead of rules, it has taken time to figure out how it can work best and with what issues. In other words, sometimes it's been rough. However, as we have learned better how to use them and apply them, those principles have given us all greater freedom. We have been able to learn how to exercise our agency in liberating ways.

[1] President Russell M. Nelson, "To be sure, there may be times when you feel as though the heavens are closed. But I promise that as you continue to be obedient, expressing gratitude for every blessing the Lord gives you, and as you patiently honor the Lord's timetable, you will be given the knowledge and understanding you seek. Every blessing the Lord has for you — even miracles — will follow. That is what personal revelation will do for you" (Revelation for the Church, Revelation for Our Lives," *Ensign*, May 2018).
[2] Elder Richard G. Scott, "Learning to Recognize Answers to Prayer," *Ensign*, Nov 1989
[3] Ether 2:19
[4] The Bible Dictionary teaches, "The object of prayer is not to change the will of God but to secure for ourselves and for others blessings that God is already willing to grant but that are made conditional on our asking for them." While this is also a true principle, the way God grants those blessings will also take many different forms (like we talked about in Chapter 2 about binding the Lord with our obedience).
[5] John Taylor, "The Organization of the Church," *Millennial Star,* Nov. 15, 1851, p. 339
[6] "Agency or Inspiration—Which?" BYU Devotional, February 27, 1973
[7] Yes, the prophets' and apostles' messages we may hear in General Conference or other means are laden with stories, experiences, and examples, but we are not necessarily meant to just get a nice, memorable story out of their message. The story is a method for communicating (and helping us remember) the much more important eternal principles we need to learn and which we can use to govern our lives in more than just that example.
[8] "Teach Them to Understand," Ricks College Campus Education Week Devotional, June 4, 1998
[9] Elder Bednar, *Increase in Learning.* (2016). Salt Lake City: Deseret Book. p. 156
[10] "Teach Them to Understand," Ricks College Campus Education Week Devotional, June 4, 1998
[11] *Preparing for an Eternal Marriage Teacher Manual*, pp. v-vii
[12] "The Word of Wisdom: A Principle with a Promise," *Ensign*, May 1996
[13] "Acquiring Spiritual Knowledge," Elder Richard G. Scott, *Ensign*, November 2009
[14] President Boyd K. Packer taught, "There is no question — personal or social or political or occupational — that need go unanswered. Therein is contained the fullness of the everlasting gospel. Therein we find principles of truth that will resolve every confusion and every problem and every dilemma that will face the human family or any individual in it." ("Teach the Scriptures," *Charge to Religious Educators*, p. 21)
[15] 1 Nephi 3:7
[16] "Heartfelt and Willing Obedience," BYU-Idaho Campus Education Week Devotional June 27, 2002

HINDRANCE #6

Making Others' Revelation Our Revelation

Let's say that a Relief Society is having a lesson one Sunday about the importance of family scripture study. And sitting in the room are these sisters:

- One sister whose busy family doesn't have scripture study consistently

- A sister with teenagers who tries to get them to participate but they won't

- Another sister whose family is pretty consistent at having scripture study

- A brand-new convert to the Church

- A sister who is struggling that day because it looks like her 18-year-old son isn't going to go on a mission and she is feeling like a failure

- A young mother whose two small children aren't old enough to study the scriptures yet

- A single sister in her 50s who is neither married nor has any children

- A grandmother who has some inactive children who are struggling and her family unit is not what she thought it would be

- A grandmother who has a very active extended family

At one point in the lesson, the teacher asks this question: "What have you done in your family that has helped you to be more consistent in studying the scriptures?" The sister in the room whose family has been consistently having scripture study raises her hand and says something like this:

"Well, we have so many different schedules in our family so, for the past several years, our family all gets up at six o'clock in the morning to study together. It wasn't easy at first, but we stuck with it and it has been an incredible experience for our family for years now. I truly believe it is the reason all four of our children have served missions."

This sister's comment was heartfelt and sincere. It included principles of gospel living and revelation that are true and valid. It contained a conclusion that may or may not have been completely the reason all four of her children served missions. Regardless, it was an honest interpretation of something that had worked for her family.

From her comment, however, it is highly probable that each sister in that room would have had very different feelings and thoughts running through their minds. How do you think the sister who was struggling to get her teenagers to participate in scripture study feels? Or the grandmother struggling with extended family?

What about the mother worrying about her 18-year-old son? She either might be feeling even wors about herself: "If only I had done that, too." Or maybe she is feeling abandoned by God: "Well, we had scripture study every day, too, and he still isn't going." Lastly, the young mother or the new convert could have been thinking: "Wow, that is exactly what I am going to do. I want all my children to serve missions, too."

These thoughts may sound familiar, or at least reasonable, to some of you. There's just one problem with every one of these conclusions: They are based on *someone else's revelation.*

Sometimes we limit revelation in our lives because we make others revelation our revelation. We hinder personal revelation in this way not only because there's actually nothing "personal" about it, but also because it's not even always *revelation* — rather it's direction someone else received, a decision they made, or it's based on an end result that someone else achieved.

To borrow another analogy, have you ever had an epic Pinterest fail where what you tried to create looked nothing like what someone else was able to create and post about? Maybe you laughed it off and just accepted that you're not as capable as someone else — or at least not as able to Photoshop as well as someone else.

Well, we can, in a sense, apply this "Pinterest Syndrome" to our lives, thinking, "That's what my life is supposed to look like, too." When we think like this, it can not only be really emotionally destructive, but it automatically sets us up for limited revelation, for this mentality severely limits the Lord's ability to speak to us *personally*. We see someone else's picture-worthy "finished product" and think it should be *ours* without spending any time figuring out what ours should really be.

A young man names James once shared with me how much he was enjoying his student ward and his new bishop. The bishop seemed like a wonderful teacher and leader, and I could tell that the young man revered him highly. James pointed out that this leader had married a beautiful woman, was a very successful accountant, had an accomplished family, lived in a very nice home, and had many possessions, including a boat that they used for ward activities. The list went on and on.

And then he surprised me. "*This*," he said to me, "is success. This is exactly what I want. And it's what I am going to work for." Through further conversations with him throughout the semester, I saw how this conclusion influenced James' schooling decisions, career choices, dating experiences, and even his faith and prayers.

We can have this mentality with so many different facets of our lives. We can see what looks on the outside to be an overflowing bank account, proven system to get a scholarship, career advancement, or successful way to raise a teenager, and think that we can and should be able to re-create what someone else has done.

However, here's the catch: often the outcomes we see in others' lives are the result of a long process we may not fully know and maybe can't even replicate. The "finished product" others create may not represent or reveal in any way, shape or form the effort, sacrifice, tears, heartache, prayer, or faith that went into it. We just don't know the whole story.

I have had many young people ask me: "What's wrong with me and with my dating life? It seems like everyone who is happily dating or engaged to be married says that I will just *know* when the person I am dating is the right one. But when I date people, I just don't seem to know if they are the one I am supposed to marry. It seems like everyone else has a 'this is the perfect one for you' meter and that mine is lost or broken or defective."

I have spent hundreds of hours throughout my career reassuring these young people that hundreds of their peers are having an identical experience; most people don't instantly discern if the one they are dating is the one they are to marry. It seems that maybe because we live in such a "broadcasted" culture, we almost by default put an incredible amount of focus on a few widely circulated stories as a measuring stick for all.

Similarly, the outward success of high achievers, or at least people achieving what we want to achieve, may not reveal the many setbacks, course changes, or waiting that was involved in their life. In short, our comparison with each other is almost always going to be skewed in some way.

Stephen R. Covey used this analogy to explain this tendency: trying to use others' knowledge, experience, or ideas to always solve our problems is like wearing their eyeglasses to correct our own vision problems because their glasses have obviously been working well for them.[1]

The sister in the family scripture study example at the beginning of this chapter had figured out what *their family* needed to do to successfully live a gospel principle. She and her husband recognized what they wanted to make happen, no matter what sacrifice it would take. They counseled together about the needs and limitations of their family. They probably also prayed about it. We have no idea how many other things they tried that didn't work. We also have no idea how long it took for their morning scripture study to be or feel successful.

All of that is because it was *their* process of revelation — a process that involved the personal application of a principle based on their understanding of a doctrine. However, that doesn't have to be *our* application of a principle based on our understanding of a doctrine!

One reason I believe we have a tendency to make others' revelation our revelation is that we misunderstand this difference between doctrines, principles, and applications. In the previous chapter, we talked about principles, and the doctrines those principles are based on: doctrines answer the "why," principles answer the "what."

Within that framework, we could ask: *Why* does the Lord counsel us to have family scripture study? One possibility is because He is an omniscient God who knows all things and has amazingly shared some of what He knows through His prophets in the scriptures.

What could be a principle we could live by (meaning what we should *do*) because of that doctrine? Feast upon those words, for the words of Christ will tell us what He knows, His plan for us, and how we can best navigate mortality (2 Nephi 32:3).

Amazing truths, aren't they? However, is there anything in what we just discussed that *specifically* tells us what "feasting upon the words of Christ" looks like? No. Does He tell us when and where and how? No. How, then, do we know how to live by a principle? Principles by nature do not usually spell out the details. That, my friends, is where *applications* come in.

Elder Bednar explained that "applications are the actual behaviors, action steps, practices, or procedures by which gospel doctrines and principles are enacted in our lives. Whereas doctrines and principles do not change, *applications appropriately can vary according to needs and circumstances*."[2]

One family's application of a principle was to wake up at six o'clock every morning and have family scripture study. That approach, however, is not the only acceptable application of that principle. As a family ponders and analyzes ways to conduct family scripture study, dozens of applicable, appropriate, and acceptable ideas might be considered that fit their family's dynamics and needs.

We need to be careful that an application does not become the doctrine or principle. For when it does, we might think we are supposed to live by it like we would a doctrine or principle. In other words, we might think that getting up at six o'clock in the morning to have family scripture study is a *doctrine*, not an application. When we separate the applications from the doctrines and principles of the gospel, we can more easily personally apply them in our lives the way the Spirit directs us and according to our needs and circumstances.

That truth is one of the great benefits of this process of identifying doctrines and principles and then learning to apply them; it gives us the opportunity to further develop the skill of receiving and acting on *revelation* rather than developing the skill of receiving and acting on specific instructions that only get us through one circumstance. This process also invites further revelation, for we must have the Spirit to further apply that revelation in our lives over and over again through our experiences.

I love how Elder Tad R. Callister ties this all together:

> "Principles tell us *what we should do*, such as to keep the Sabbath day holy or feast upon the word of God, but the Holy Ghost teaches us *how to apply a given principle* in a given circumstance — how to keep the Sabbath day holy or how to feast upon the word of God. Principles and the Holy Ghost work in tandem— teaching us the correct doctrinal truth and how to apply it. A principle without the Holy Ghost becomes no more than a sterile or mechanical guideline. On the other hand, the Holy Ghost without principles may be restricted in His ability to direct us. The more we understand and embrace eternal principles, the greater room and flexibility we give the Holy Ghost to help us apply such principles to specific situations in our lives."[3]

I don't know about you, but these truths make me rejoice! What a great God we worship! He truly does honor our agency. He truly does allow us to grow into understanding as we gain more knowledge and experience. He allows us to figure out what living a certain principle or applying a doctrine is going to look like in our lives. All are incredible opportunities to have experiences with the Spirit. He also acknowledges our differences — not just in geography or culture, but in personalities and limitations. We are trusted with our own process.

In that freedom and trust, however, I believe that also means that we are accountable for that application. We are accountable to seek ways that we might be ready or able to apply things in more divine and holy ways in our lives. This concept of personal application doesn't get us off the hook: "Well, in our family the application of this principle is that we are not going to read the scriptures because we are too busy." Remember, righteous application involves the behavior, actions, or practices that represent the depth of our belief and faith in the doctrines and principles of the gospel.

Do you remember when we talked earlier about looking to the horizontal in our lives? I wonder if this hindrance might be another way we do that. We look to others' answers and make them ours, instead of looking to heaven for them.

I've had a few personal experiences with this concept. For example, I have a wonderful daughter who is as obedient as they come, but who really doesn't like making decisions. As she was growing up, when I would tell her what she should do in a particular situation, she would usually just happily and obediently do it. What a joy she was! There were even times when she would beg me, "Just tell me what I should do. I don't want to make the decision." And for a while, I would do just that — I would tell her what to do.

However, over the years I realized something: I wasn't helping her! Why? Because I was a horizontal source in her life and, in reality, my role is not to be her unfailing source of guidance and wisdom and comfort. When it comes down to it, my role as a parent is to point her vertically.

Now, hopefully, I'm a good horizontal source in her life. Hopefully, I am someone my children can turn to, someone who is a good example to them. However, I am still a horizontal source. I make mistakes. I won't always be there for them when and how they need it. My own false beliefs and biases can influence my direction for them.

Besides, is their existence on this planet to see if they can find *me* amid the noise and confusion? Is it to love *me* even when they feel abandoned, to trust *me* to guide their next step into the dark? Not really. They need to learn to find and love and trust and look *to God*.

This reality seems to apply to even the best sources in our lives. If I were to ask you if the prophet is a horizontal or vertical source, what would you say? Many, at first, instantly answer that the prophet is a vertical source. However, in reality, he's actually a horizontal one. He's impressively close to the vertical, but even the prophets themselves say they are not to be our source of revelation. Their voices are simply being *His* voice as His message is carried to our hearts by the Spirit.[4]

Elder Neil L. Anderson of the Quorum of Twelve Apostles taught, "The prophet does not stand between you and the Savior. Rather, he stands beside you and points the way to the Savior."[5] Moses, a prophet who was constantly burdened by a people who would not turn to God themselves, also pleaded, "Would God that all the Lord's people were prophets, and that the Lord would put His spirit upon them!" implying that each of us needs to have our own experiences with revelation (Numbers 11:29).

I believe an experience from Elder Marion G. Romney's life also reiterates this truth. Elder Romney once struggled with something the Brethren had taught, a political stance that he didn't agree with, and, as he was working through it, he shared this with President Harold B. Lee: "I knew what I should do — but that wasn't enough. I knew that I must feel right about following the counsel of the Church leaders *and know that they were right*. That took a whole night on my knees to accomplish."[6]

At that time, Elder Romney was a member of the Quorum of the Twelve Apostles, and yet he needed to spend a night on his knees for a personal witness that what the Brethren had said was right. If he had to work that hard for a witness from God, it seems we should not be surprised if we sometimes might have to do the same.

I'll never forget an experience Michelle had with this principle many years ago. She had called a good and trusted friend who was also the mother of a large family to ask her a question about their media standards. After Michelle posed her question, the other mother gave a few thoughts and ideas about what they had done and some principles they had used to make their decisions.

Then, almost mid-conversation, this wise mother said, "But, Michelle, it doesn't matter what we do. It doesn't matter what we have done. You need to figure out what is right for your little family. Heavenly Father knows your kids. I don't. He will guide you with what standards you need to set and then He will help you navigate through it. You'll do great!"[7] And that was that.

We are expected to receive our own revelation and are accountable for the revelation *we* receive. Thankfully, how one family got out of debt does not have to be our family's journey. What one mother decides to do to monitor her children's cell phones may not work for our family. How one retired couple chose to continue building up God's kingdom may not be our best route. When we take the burden of having to do and be like everyone else off of our shoulders, life just isn't as heavy.

As we understand this process of applying doctrines and principles better in our lives, we use revelation better in our lives. We step up and take responsibility for the work we must do to get our own answer. We more prayerfully and sincerely seek the guidance He is willing to give. We have more confidence that it truly will be what Elder Neal A. Maxwell calls "customized curriculum."[8]

Here are some examples of what that customized curriculum could look like in our family scripture study example:

> One sister being inspired to improve their already fairly consistent scripture study by asking each of her children to direct the discussion.

> Another receiving divine assurance that her efforts, as pitiful as they may seem on the outside, are exactly what is expected of her right then.

The new convert being taught a way to slowly implement family study on Sundays.

Another being inspired to do some prayerful searching of what might work for her resistant teenagers.

One mother being given some personal and meaningful insights into how she could help her son who was struggling with going on a mission — insights, no less, that really had nothing to do with the discussion they were having in that Relief Society lesson.

The single sister feeling impressed to study the scriptures with a good friend once a week.

Regardless of their situation, each sister could receive guidance that would meet the needs in her life. Again, because our lives are all so different, we not only cannot compare ourselves to each other, but we also cannot assume that another person's inspiration is going to fit with our circumstances. Even with similar experiences, our journey is not going to be like anyone else's journey. Often, neither will our outcomes.

Elder Larry Y. Wilson of the Seventy shared that, when considering Lehi's vision, he could envision "throngs of people traveling that path, some with their hands firmly gripping the iron rod, but many others simply following the feet of the people in front of them. This latter approach takes little thought or effort. . . . This works fine in sunny weather. But the storms of deception and the mists of falsehood arise without warning. In these situations, being familiar with the voice of the Holy Ghost is a matter of spiritual life and death. . . . Following the feet of the people ahead of you on the path is not enough. We cannot just do and think about what others are doing and thinking; we must live a guided life."[9]

As a balancing principle, this isn't to say we shouldn't or can't ever rely on others for guidance or support. President Spencer W. Kimball taught that God often works through other people to meet our needs.[10] There may be times that He gives us needed insight through the words or experiences of someone else. Sometimes, something shared in

Church can be the very answer to prayer we have been seeking for months. A feeling to seek out someone who has gone through similar experiences may be the Lord's nudging. Others' insight and help can be inspired, even delivered straight from God; they can be His messengers.

However they are delivered, the Lord has very individual messages that each of us can and need to hear — sometimes that have nothing to do with what is being taught or shared and read in the moment. We need the power of this individual instruction in our lives. He loves and knows each one of us so perfectly and intimately that He knows what we are capable of, need, and want. We just need to be constantly checking in with Him. So, let's just be careful that we do not become tossed to and fro with every wind of others' application of a doctrine or principle. Let's be careful not to compare and, in that comparison, expect the same thing of ourselves that others have accomplished or been directed to do.

We are not responsible for what others have done, nor are we responsible for what the Lord told someone else to do. We are only responsible for figuring out what *we* are supposed to do. We are only responsible for making sure our efforts are validated by the Lord. Indeed, we just have to make sure that what we decide to do, what we decide to say, where we decide to go, or how we decide to live is, in the end, *our* revelation.

Therefore, What?

Expect "Word of Wisdom" lessons. As you consider ways that you might be hindering revelation in your life by making others' revelation your revelation, I first encourage you to watch for "Word of Wisdom Lessons" as you go through your experiences. Expect to receive the "customized curriculum" the Lord has prepared for you that might be different (or at least more personalized) than what He has prepared for someone else. Approach every lesson, every car ride, every class, every conversation, every scripture study, every meeting, and even every trip through the checkout line with the expectation that

God can and will teach you the things *you* need for *your* life if you listen and watch for them.

Begin to identify the doctrine, principles, and applications in your life. Also, maybe take some time to evaluate how you are using doctrines, principles, and applications in your life. What doctrine does a rule in your family stem from? Can you identify the doctrine behind a principle you are living? Also, what principles are you basing your decisions on? Why should you pray? Why should we be obedient? Do your children know *why* the Lord commands us to keep the Sabbath holy? What principle are you trying to teach your teenager daughter that might not have anything to do with the length of her shorts or how much of her shoulder her sleeve covers? Knowing the "why" and the "what" helps us figure out "how."

These recognitions help us better find the applications of those principles and doctrines. I wonder if sometimes we adopt others' applications simply because we don't even know what principle we are trying to live by in the first place.

President Spencer W. Kimball once taught, "Jesus operated from a base of fixed principles or truths rather than making up the rules as he went along. . . . [He] knew who he was and why he was here on this planet. That meant he could lead from strength rather than from uncertainty or weakness."[11]

As we begin to recognize and acknowledge the doctrine and principles behind our everyday applications of those doctrines and principles, we can not only act and lead with much more strength, but also be much more likely to receive revelation. Truth lines us up with the conduits of heaven. Our reasoning behind what we do is based on something eternal instead of someone's opinion or someone else's revelation.

How might this change how I counsel others or share experiences? We can also apply this principle to the opportunities we have to lead, teach, and counsel others. We can ask ourselves: Do I share my opinion too quickly or so often that it prevents someone else from turning to the Lord for answers? Do I share revelation I have received with someone with a similar issue as an answer for them?

Here are some questions we can begin to ask instead:

"Have you gone to the Lord?"

"What has the Lord told you to do?"

"What have *you* felt about it?"

These questions are also helpful to ask ourselves for our church classes and discussions: When I comment in Sunday School, am I trying to share my testimony of a principle or am I trying to encourage everyone else in the room to do as I did? Do the sisters in our Relief Society understand that one person's comment about what they were inspired to do is not necessarily a revelation for everyone? The more we understand what we are testifying of — whether it's a doctrine, principle, or application — the more we bless others and learn from others.

---

[1] *"The 7 Habits of Highly Effective People."*

[2] *Increase in Learning,* p. 156, emphasis added; Church policy also seems to be an application of doctrines and principles. Nothing eternal changed when the Church changed the missionary age. Just the procedure for calling missionaries.

[3] "The Power of Principles," 1st Annual LDS Educators Conference, BYU, July 15, 2017

[4] D&C 1:38

[5] "The Prophet of God," *Ensign*, May 2018

[6] Robert L. Millett, *Magnifying Priesthood Power*. (2008). Springville, Utah: Horizon p. 109, emphasis added

[7] Advice from Kathleen Johnson Thatcher, mother of 13

[8] Elder Neal A. Maxwell, "He will customize the curriculum for each of us in order to teach us the things we most need to know. He will set before us in life what we need, not always what we like. And this will require us to accept with all our hearts—particularly your generation—the truth that there is divine design in each of our lives and that you have a rendezvous to keep, individually and collectively." ("But for a Small Moment," BYU Devotional, September 1, 1974)

[9] "Take the Holy Spirit as Your Guide," *Ensign,* May 2018

[10] "God does notice us, and he watches over us. But it is usually through another person that he meets our needs. Therefore, it is vital that we serve each other in the kingdom. The people of the Church need each other's strength, support, and leadership in a community of believers as an enclave of disciples." (*Teachings of Presidents of the Church: Spencer W. Kimball,* (2006), pp. 79 — 88)

[11] "Jesus: The Perfect Leader," *Ensign,* August, 1979

HINDRANCE #7

Having an Encumbered Mind

Years ago, I got a priesthood blessing for some direction. There were some decisions I needed to make that I just couldn't get clarity on. In that blessing, an interesting set of phrases stood out to me: "Stephen, you are cumbered about much. There are some things you must get rid of so that you can be guided better, focus more, and choose more wisely."

I recognized the phrase "cumbered about much" from the account of Mary and Martha in the New Testament. Jesus had come to their village and Martha had received him into her house. While He was there, Mary sat at His feet and listened to His teachings, while Martha "cumbered about much serving" (Luke 10:40).

Think about the fuss we often make when we host visitors in our home. Can you imagine the pressure of hosting the Savior? I'm not sure that Martha didn't care about what the Savior was teaching, but rather that she was simply concerned about being a good hostess — maybe making sure her guest was comfortable, attending to a meal for Him, or cleaning up a little bit.

But after a while, Martha said to Jesus, "Lord, dost thou not care that my sister hath left me to serve alone? Bid her therefore that she help me. And Jesus answered and said unto her, "Martha, Martha, thou art careful and troubled about many things: But one thing is needful: and Mary hath chosen that good part" (vs. 40-41).

After I received that blessing, I went home and asked Michelle what things might be encumbering me and what things I might need to eliminate from my life. She suggested I look up how "encumbered" is defined. I discovered it means to weigh down or burden, or to obstruct or inhibit the function of something. This definition seemed to imply to me that being encumbered means we are distracted by unnecessary pursuits or burdened with unnecessary things.

Once I started to understand all that this counsel could mean, I sat down and listed every demand on my time: my job, my priesthood calling, my commitments as a husband, father, son, neighbor, and friend. Pretty much everything on that list seemed important and appropriate and in line with the principles of the gospel. I couldn't figure out what I was supposed to cut out.

I pondered over the next few weeks what on my list might be an unnecessary pursuit or burden. Should I not coach my son's basketball team anymore? Should I ask to be released from the bishopric? Was I too busy at work? None of those seemed to be the answer.

A few weeks later, we went to watch my son run in a mile race for all the 5th graders in our area. As we were getting ready to leave for the race, one of our daughters spontaneously decided to come watch the race even though she had to be to work a short while later.

All of a sudden my mind started going crazy worrying that she would never make it to work on time if she came to the race and that if she didn't make it to work on time, then she was going to get in trouble at work or even get fired. I immediately started figuring out the exact time she would need to leave to get there when she needed. When we got to the race, I think I stressed more about watching my watch and calculating the time that she needed to leave than watching my son race and celebrating he had shaved a few seconds off of his best time.

Then these thoughts came in quick succession into my mind: "This is what I'm talking about. You are encumbered *in your mind.* You worry about other people and their agency. You think about what's going to happen because of choices made right now. It is a gift you have and is good at times, but it can also a hindrance to receiving revelation. You analyze circumstances, dwell on things that have happened at work, and think about so many things that I cannot talk to you. Your mind is going so fast and so far down the road. It is so weighed down."

There was my answer. It wasn't that I was *doing* too much. I was worrying too much, thinking too much, stressing too much, all of which was making it very difficult for the Lord to tell me in my mind through the Holy Ghost what I should do.[1] I also realized it wasn't necessarily that my mind was focused on bad things or worldly things, but rather that it was simply so busy thinking about *a lot* of things it was difficult to also discern the direction I was seeking from the heavens.

I have discovered that being encumbered or feeling scattered by all the different directions we are trying to go overpowers the whisper of the "still small voice" (D&C 85:6). Sometimes, the Spirit just can't compete.[2] Sister Sheri Dew observed, "We can allow the distractions and pace of our lives to crowd out the Spirit. . . . No wonder that one of the adversary's favorite tactics among righteous LDS women (and men, I might add) is busyness . . ."[3]

There are definitely things we can simplify in our lives to make room for the Spirit, but there are also things we can simplify in our *minds* so that there is room for the Spirit.

Once I realized it was my encumbered mind that was preventing me from receiving the revelation I needed, I went back to the story of Mary and Martha. I noticed a few things I hadn't noticed before. First, the record says Mary "heard his word" (Luke 10:39). It seems she was able to hear what the Lord was teaching — eternal things that could not be taken from her — because she had removed all other distractions and sat at His feet. That may not be profound but, in this context, its significance stood out to me: we have to make room for revelation.

President Boyd K. Packer taught, "The mind is like a stage. During every waking moment, the curtain is up. There is always some act being performed on that stage. It may be a comedy, a tragedy, interesting or dull, good or bad; but always there is some act playing on the stage of your mind."[4] And, according to President Ezra Taft Benson, there's only room for one act to be on that stage at any given time. We have to decide what is going to play out on that stage. We decide what thoughts we will accept.[5]

That decision, by default, not only involves what we are going to focus on in any given situation but how much space is left for the promptings of the Spirit. One woman realized, "I'm not very good at asking the Lord if there's anything He needs me to do that day because I usually already have my day planned out before I ever get out of bed. I can't imagine it's very easy for Him to insert something in when my mind is not really seeking His insight."

Luke records that Jesus then said to Martha, "Thou art careful and troubled about many things." Two interesting verbs: *careful* and *troubled*. Martha was serving. It wasn't that she was doing bad things. She was trying to be helpful. She was *careful* — or, in a sense, "full of care" — focusing on and attending to the needs of others because she cared about them. In fact, I wondered if it may have simply been her personality to like to take care of things around her, much like mine is.

But look at the second verb: *troubled*. It seems it is also very easy for our *care* about something to turn into being *troubled* by it. In fact, our minds can be unnecessarily troubled with many things besides the choices of others.

For example, we can worry about what *isn't* happening in our lives — becoming consumed with the attention we *aren't* getting, the opportunities that never seem to be ours, the job given to someone else, or the children who haven't come back to the gospel. This focus on the lack in our lives can prevent us from seeing not only the abundance in our lives but the abundant mercy and peace and wisdom the Lord is pouring into our lives.

We can become consumed with *being* right instead of discerning what *is* right, or pleasing others instead of pleasing the Lord. Indeed, we can worry so much about our standing with others or how our lives compare to theirs that we fall prey to what Elder Jeffrey R. Holland described as "our culture's obsession with comparing, competing and never feeling like we are 'enough.'"[6] A mind focused on keeping up with everyone might not have the energy to focus on keeping the commandments and covenants that qualify us for the Spirit.

One other principle I learned from the Savior's visit to Mary and Martha's home was much more subtle. Mary had decided to sit and listen to the Savior. Martha, on the other hand, had decided to take care of many things. The Savior didn't say anything about either of their choices . . . that is until Martha complained: "Lord dost thou not care that my sister hath left me to serve alone?" Martha was worried about what Mary wasn't doing. *And that's what it seems the Lord corrected her on.* He corrected Martha's worrying about Mary's choices, not about what she, herself, had chosen to do.

Is it possible that Jesus wasn't worried so much about Martha serving while He was teaching because He knew that she could still learn from Him while she was serving? But if her mind was encumbered with what someone else was choosing to do, she possibly couldn't learn as well from Him. My list of what I was doing in my life seemed to be in line with what God wanted me to do, but the focus of my mind was distracting me.

Worry, as opposed to *concern*, is often caused by things that we can't do anything about.[7] Most of the choices others make are not within our ability to control. One young missionary wisely shared: "I think one of Satan's greatest tools is to make us stress about the things that are out of our control. Why? Because it causes us to waste a tremendous amount of time and it makes us feel constantly inadequate." Being troubled by these things also fills our minds with unnecessary fear and anxiety — both emotions that hinder revelation.

For example, as parents, we can worry so much about how a child is using their agency, there isn't room for the Lord to guide us on how to guide them with that agency; or better yet, there isn't room for the Lord to teach us about *our* agency. We might micromanage, interfere with that agency, or even lose sight of the person themselves because we are so focused on their problem. We can become so concerned about what *they* are doing, we can't discern what *we* should be doing.

The Savior instructed Martha that one thing was "needful" in that moment and that Mary had chosen the more needful part. Some of what we think or worry about may be important, it just might not be as important as what the Lord may be trying to tell us in that moment. Our job, it seems, then is to figure out what is needful in the moment. Michelle has shared with me, as I'm sure many of you have felt, that sometimes she chooses not to add something else to her plate simply because she can't handle the mental energy it requires, not necessarily because she doesn't have time.

Elder Joseph B. Wirthlin once shared: "Sometimes we feel the busier we are, the more important we are, as though our busyness defines our worth. . . . That we do a lot may not be so important. That we focus the energy of our minds, our hearts, and our souls on those things of eternal significance — that is essential."[8]

This life is busy and distracting and overwhelming at times. We are bombarded with a lot of information on a daily basis. There's no way around some of that. However, our minds can become encumbered with it if we allow it to consume the stage. Indeed, it would not surprise me if some of the adversary's intent in tempting us to connect our worth to busyness or chasing things that seem important is also so that our minds will either be too full or just completely worn out to discern the things of God.

Paul admonished the Philippians, "Be careful for nothing; but in every thing by prayer and supplication with thanksgiving let your requests be made known unto God. And the peace of God, which passeth all understanding, shall keep your hearts and minds through Christ Jesus" (Philippians 4:6-7).

In Greek, the phrase "be careful for nothing" is another way of saying, "Don't get overanxious about things. Don't worry so much." We can be filled with peace and every other fruit of the Spirit when we choose through Christ's power to keep our minds in check. We can discern better, hear more clearly, and understand better what God is trying to give us.

Paul then offered the Saints in Philippi some things we, too, can ponder on. He counseled them to think on whatsoever is true, honest, just, pure, lovely, of good report, virtuous, or praiseworthy; think about those things that they had both learned, and received, and heard, and seen.[9]

Truth, honesty, virtue, praise, purity, and other positive thoughts do not encumber the mind; they do not crowd out revelation. Instead, they *invite* revelation. The Lord has promised He will expand and enlighten our minds.[10] They can be enlightened with the things of eternity that are never a burden. His "yoke is easy" and His "burden is light" compared to the burden of the cares of the world (Matthew 11: 28-30).

Therefore, What?

What's taking up precious space on the stage of your mind? As you think about ways revelation could be being hindered from an encumbered mind, heart, or life, consider first what things in your life might be consuming your mental stage. What worry is running on replay in the back of your mind all the time? Whose troubles come to mind when you first wake in the morning? How many times today have you thought about the hurtful thing your friend or coworker or spouse said to you last week? What did you stress about yesterday that caused you to tune out a task at hand, others around you, or even the Spirit?

Also consider this: Is the sin of competing with others, comparing your life to others' lives, or never feeling like you are doing enough, going fast enough, or being enough robbing you not only of peace of mind, but of some great spiritual experiences?

Determining good, better, best. Did you notice what Martha was "cumbered about much" doing? She was *serving*. She was doing something good. It seems one of the challenges of this life is that we must make daily and sometimes hourly decisions. Yes, we must make choices between good and bad. But we can become encumbered with good, meaningful, and righteous endeavors if we are not careful — a principle shared by Elder Dallin H. Oaks in a Conference address entitled "Good, Better, Best."[11] Sometimes, good and better choices can make us too tired or too distracted to discern the most "needful" thing in our lives.

How do we free up the mind? There are many ways we can clear out space for revelation in our minds. Here are a few suggestions.

First, find the antidote. I've noticed a pattern the Lord often uses for correcting and changing things. He teaches us about the *antidote*, or what will help counteract the unwanted "poison" on our lives. Faith is the antidote to fear.[12] Humility is the antidote to pride. Work is the antidote to worry and anxiety.[13]

In fact, this approach seems to be one of the underlying principles in President Packer's teaching about understanding true doctrine. He taught, "The study of the doctrines of the gospel will improve behavior quicker than a study of behavior will improve behavior. *Preoccupation with unworthy behavior can lead to unworthy behavior.* That is why we stress so forcefully the study of the doctrines of the gospel.[14] Thus, it seems, for example, we don't get rid of our pride by focusing on our pride; we, instead, focus on understanding, seeking after, and developing the humility the Savior exemplified.

What might be an antidote to the tendency of being stressed or having a burdened mind? There are probably many. One that I've discovered is gratitude. A grateful mind is very seldom an encumbered mind. I'm not completely sure how it works, but gratitude seems to have almost a magical effect on everything. When we are grateful, it brings clarity, removes distractions, and helps us focus on spiritual thoughts that are higher than our thoughts.

Secondly, allow time for your pattern of thinking to change. Because of my own experiences trying to free up an encumbered mind, I know changing patterns of thinking is not necessarily easy. Often, I'm already well into my familiar habit of worrying about something before I'm conscious of it! Some well-meaning friends may say, "Well, just don't go there. Just don't worry about it." But it's not always that easy — especially for the things that are individually difficult for each one of us.

It takes a deliberate effort of re-learning how to handle stressful situations or unexpected circumstances. It takes a conscious choice of faith over fear. And often, it is much more about preventing the worry process from continuing once we've "already gone there." Regardless of what we must do, I have found that, often, we must involve prayer in this "unencumbering effort." When I recognize that I've allowed the wheels in my head to start spinning again, I pray very specifically for help to resolve it, put it in perspective, divert it, shut it off, or simply ignore it. Sincere, faithful prayer connects me to Christ, and then He helps me figure out what must be done.

_____

_____

_____

_____

_____

_____

_____

_____

[1] D&C 8:2

[2] D&C 85:6

[3] "We Are Not Alone," *Ensign*, November 1998

[4] "Worthy Thoughts, Worthy Music," *New Era*, April 2008

[5] "Think On Christ," *Ensign*, April 1984: "The mind has been compared to a stage on which only one act at a time can be performed. From one side of the wings the Lord, who loves you, is trying to put on the stage of your mind that which will bless you. From the other side of the wings the devil, who hates you, is trying to put on the stage of your mind that which will curse you. You are the stage manager—you are the one who decides which thought will occupy the stage. Remember, the Lord wants you to have a fullness of joy like His. The devil wants all men to be miserable like him. You are the one who must decide which thoughts you will accept. You are free to choose—but you are not free to alter the results of those choices. You will be what you think about—what you consistently allow to occupy the stage of your mind."

[6] Elder Jeffrey R. Holland, "The Tongue of Angels," *Ensign*, May 2007

[7] Elder Richard G. Scott shares a powerful example in a talk called, "The Comforting Circle of True Friendship" about a time in his life when he had to learn how to discern between concerns and worry. It is found in the *Ensign*, July 1983.

[8] "Follow Me," *Ensign*, May 2002

[9] vs. 8-9

[10] D&C 6:15, 11:13; Alma 32:34

[11] *Ensign*, November 2007

[12] "God Hath Not Given Us the Spirit of Fear," *Ensign*, October 1984; Elder Russell M. Nelson, "Let Your Faith Show," *Ensign*, May 2014

[13] President Hinckley, "Put Your Shoulder to the Wheel," *Ensign*, July 2000; Elder Dieter F. Uchtdorf, "Two Principles for Any Economy," *Ensign*, November 2009

[14] "Little Children," *Ensign,* November 1986; emphasis added

HINDRANCE #8

Giving Reasons to Revelation Part I

I used to teach Institute in the Washington, D.C. area. I loved the environment there in Northern Virginia with its historical and military influence, but I especially loved the students! They were a bright, fun, and amazing group of individuals. Many were college graduates between the ages of about 24 and 30 who had moved there to work in some kind of government or military facet, and about 70% of them were female.

Often I would ask, "So, why Washington D.C.? What brought you out here?" Some would say a job or that they knew there was a lot of single LDS people in that area. More often than not, however, when I would ask that question, this is what I would get: "I don't know. I just had a feeling to come here." As I would look into their faces, especially the girls, there would be almost a twinkle in their eyes. And I came to learn what that twinkle usually meant: "I think I'm going to find my husband here."

I would then watch an interesting thing happen throughout the semester: many of them would begin to struggle. They became frustrated or depressed. They would pull away from the ward, sometimes stop coming to Institute.

As I would reach out to them to see what I could do to help, this is what they would share: "Two years ago God told me to come here so I could get married. It obviously hasn't happened. In fact, I hardly even date. I'm totally confused. I'm not sure if I was even supposed to come here."

Because this happened often enough, I became familiar with walking them through this series of questions:

"What were the impressions you received when you first felt to come here. What was your experience like?"

Their stories and experiences would usually differ, but somewhere in their sharing they would say something like this: "Well, I don't know. I just felt I needed to move here." or "I received a priesthood blessing and it said I needed to come here."

I would then ask, "In the midst of those feelings, did the Lord specifically tell you that the reason He was sending you here was that you were going to get married?"

After sitting and thinking for a moment, many would realize, "No, I don't think so."

"So, where could that have come from?" I would ask.

"Well . . . I'm not sure," they might say. "I don't really know." And some would even ask, "Could I have added that myself?"

As we would continue to talk through it, many would indeed realize they had somehow added that reason themselves.

In all honesty, I couldn't blame them. Finding someone to share their lives with is a righteous desire. The marriage covenant is something they have been taught to look forward to, rejoice in, and actively seek. Yet, what I think often happened is that they had mixed up the revelation to move to Washington D.C. with some impatience, misunderstanding, maybe some loneliness or insecurity, and all of those hopes, dreams, and righteous desires.[1]

The result? They thought they knew the reason they should move. However, many of them would discover it wasn't necessarily God's reason for them to move. Without meaning to, they did this:

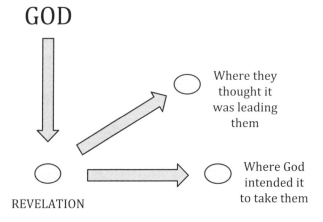

GOD

Where they thought it was leading them

REVELATION

Where God intended it to take them

Their experience is an example of another way we can hinder revelation in our lives: by "giving reason" to it. This hindrance basically involves jumping to our own mortal conclusions or adding our own meaning or interpretation to the promptings that God gives.

The danger in these interpretations is that they can distort the direction we've already received. They can also take that revelation in a completely different direction than it was meant to go, even going so far as to inhibit further revelation. Indeed, our interpretations can even alter a revelation to the point where it becomes completely wrong.

A recently returned senior missionary once shared with me another example of what this can look like. While serving with his wife on their mission, Brother Langford would sometimes have the opportunity to give the missionaries priesthood blessings. One time, he was giving an elder a blessing right before he was to return home. As he was in the middle of the blessing, he could see in his mind a wonderful young woman with blond hair and felt there was something important about her. In fact, he was pretty sure it was the young man's future wife.

When he concluded the blessing, however, Brother Langford felt to simply tell the young man to go home and prepare himself diligently for the next step in his life. Many months later, this senior missionary saw on the young man's social media account the young woman from the vision. He was surprised to discover it was the young man's *sister*.

It was then that he realized he had assumed he knew who the young woman was and had misinterpreted what the vision had meant. This faithful brother had no intention of giving reason to that revelation. Thankfully, he chose not to say anything specific to the elder at the time, but what an eye-opening experience it was for him.

Have you ever done something like this? Have you felt a prompting and immediately started trying to figure out what it means? Were you instructed to do something and instantly wanted to figure out why? Sometimes blessings come and we immediately think we know why the Lord blessed us. Or we receive a calling and assume we know the reason that we specifically were called to it.

I'm not completely sure all the reasons we do this, but I think one could possibly be that we think we are *supposed* to. We believe it is our responsibility to know, or at least make an effort to figure out, the "why" behind the Lord's working in our lives. Indeed, it almost feels wrong not to at least do *something* after we receive an impression. (Isn't it interesting how the adversary will interfere with inspiration in whatever way he can, including planting misunderstanding in our minds about our role in it?)

We could also do this because of impatience or curiosity or the need to at least make sense of something in our lives. However, I'm thinking, more often than not, it is because of the false belief that being "anxiously engaged" means we are also supposed to use our agency to "run" with or explain revelation we receive.

And sometimes, it's so hard not to, especially when we receive a distinct impression — even just a few words, or a short phrase — and then nothing else for a while, no explanation whatsoever. "Don't take that class." We follow it, thinking it must have been because it would have been too hard or unnecessary. "Ask him how he's doing." We ask, assuming we are asking because the Lord wants us to help him with something. "Tell her you are not going to force her to go to church," thinking that impression must mean she might choose to go on her own. It is very difficult to not try to figure out what an impression means or why the Lord prompted us in that way.

Elder Dallin H. Oaks once shared a powerful statement that gives insight not only into why we are not expected to interpret revelation but also why we shouldn't. He said:

> "If you read the scriptures with this question in mind, 'Why did the Lord command this or why did he command that,' you find that in less than one in a hundred commands was any reason given. It's not the pattern of the Lord to give reasons. We [mortals] can put reasons to revelation. We can put reasons to commandments. When we do, we're on our own.
>
> "Some people put reasons to [the priesthood ban] and they turned out to be spectacularly wrong. There is a lesson in that. . . . The lesson I've drawn from that, I decided a long time ago that I had faith in the command and I had no faith in the reasons that had been suggested for it. . . . I'm referring to

reasons given by general authorities and reasons elaborated upon [those reasons] by others. The whole set of reasons seemed to me to be unnecessary risk taking. . . . Let's [not] make the mistake that's been made in the past, here and in other areas, trying to put reasons to revelation. The reasons turn out to be man-made to a great extent. The revelations are what we sustain as the will of the Lord and that's where safety lies."[2]

Even though Elder Oaks was referring specifically to the priesthood ban in these remarks, he is teaching a valuable principle here that I believe can be applied to many other experiences we have with revelation: when we give a reason — or in other words, *our limited, mortal opinion* — for a revelation given to us by God, we can often be spectacularly wrong.

And one reason could be because of what we can't see.

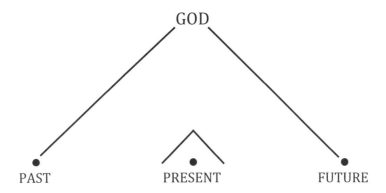

GOD

PAST   PRESENT   FUTURE

Imagine that the little dot above the word "present" in this diagram is each one of us. The triangle over us represents the limit of what we can see and understand as a mortal here on earth.[3] The triangle starting at the top and coming down from God symbolizes what He can see and understand.

How much can we see? Not a lot.

But, what can God see? Everything. All things are present before His eyes.[4] The past, present, and future. And not just of our lives, but of the whole earth and every person who has been or ever will live on the earth. He can see and comprehend it all. He has no limitations.[5] Thus, His ways are literally higher than our ways, His thoughts higher than our thoughts.[6]

Looking at this simple diagram through the lens of understanding revelation, it becomes obvious why revelation is such a crucial component of our experience here on earth. But it also becomes obvious why we would be foolish to try and interpret the full ramifications of its divine meaning.

Elder Bruce R. McConkie observed that the Jews during the time of Christ "took the plain and simple things of pure religion and added to them *a host of their own interpretations*; they embellished them with added rites and performances; and they took a happy, joyous way of worship and turned it into a restrictive, curtailing, depressive system of rituals and performances."[7]

Sometimes, our own interpretations can become bondage just like the Law of Moses. In fact, I wonder if that's what those wonderful young sisters in D.C. were really experiencing: bondage to an expectation that was seriously limiting their understanding and robbing them of what could have been a happy, joyous once-in-a-lifetime experience. Elder Richard G. Scott called these the "dead ends" of our own reasoning.[8]

In the Old Testament, we learn about Joseph, the son of Jacob, and his experience with interpreting dreams. One of those experiences involved a baker and a butler. When they each asked him if he would tell them the meaning of their strange dreams, he said, "Interpretations belong to God" (Genesis 40:8). Joseph then shared with them his *inspired* conclusions — one of them would live and the other would be hanged.

Yet, the butler must not have fully understood how that whole process worked. For over two years later, Pharaoh himself was troubled by a dream and said to Joseph, "I have heard say of thee (obviously from that butler who survived), that thou canst understand a dream to interpret it." Joseph corrected Pharaoh by saying, "*'It is not in me*: God shall give Pharaoh an answer of peace'" (41:15-16, emphasis added).

Joseph, it seems, understood just how small his triangle was. He realized that he didn't have the knowledge or experience to fully understand what the Lord meant by the dream, nor what His further direction would be because of it. It was an idea that involved God's higher thoughts and purposes from His eternal perspective. Joseph seemed to know that God is His own interpreter; He chooses if and when He will make His purposes known.[9]

In the process, as the Lord gave Joseph divine insight into the meaning of those dreams, He also expanded his understanding. He enlightened Joseph with more knowledge than he had before. In a sense, He lifted his triangle a little bit.

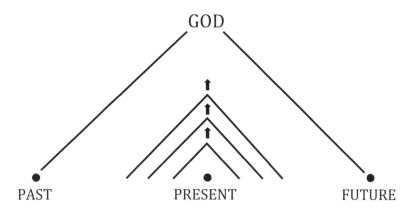

As we receive God's higher thoughts and gain more divine understanding, our triangle seems to actually be lifted and expanded. We can't push it up with our own strength. However when we reach up to God and seek His wisdom, He enlightens our understanding and expands our vision, and lifts our eyes, until one distant day we will actually be able to see what He sees.[10]

One of my students added this incredible insight to this visual: "The amazing thing about this concept is that when God does allow us to see, He increases our understanding by *enlarging our capacity* to see what He sees, rather than trying to cram more stuff into our tiny triangle of perspective. But it seems, even then, that He cares much more about our ability to develop a relationship with Him and trust Him than our ability to always understand the way He sees things at this time in our lives."

Years ago, I started noticing a pattern in the experiences of President Thomas S. Monson. Often he would feel impressed to go visit someone without knowing exactly why, or what he was going to say or do once he got there.

He shares one particularly poignant story about receiving a distinct prompting to go visit a good friend in the hospital who had recently lost the use of his legs from illness and surgery. He immediately set out for the hospital. When he arrived, the man was not in his room. After searching the hospital, he found him sitting in his wheelchair on the edge of the pool near the deep end.

President Monson shares, "I called to him, and he maneuvered his wheelchair over to greet me. We had an enjoyable visit, and I accompanied him back to his hospital room, where I gave him a blessing. I learned later from my friend that he had been utterly despondent that day and had been contemplating taking his own life. He had prayed for relief but began to feel that his prayers had gone unanswered. He went to the pool with the thought that this would be a way to end his misery — by guiding his wheelchair into the deep end of the pool. I had arrived at a critical moment, in response to what I know was inspiration from on high."[11]

It seems the Lord didn't give President Monson the end with the beginning. He did not tell him, "Go to the hospital right now because your friend is about to take his life." He just prompted him to go. And when the Lord prompted him to go, Thomas Monson moved — much like Nephi, who was led by the Spirit, "not knowing beforehand" all the things the Lord would have him do.[12]

It seems President Monson also knew, as Joseph of Egypt did, that interpretations belong to God. His life was full of experiences where the Lord's purposes could be accomplished because he *acted* on the inspiration and impressions that came to him without knowing all the details and without having to know the reasons behind why he was acting.

This kind of faith reminds me of the message in the wonderful hymn "Lead, Kindly Light:"

"Lead, kindly Light amid th'encircling gloom;
Lead thou me on!
The night is dark, and I am far from home;
Lead thou me on!
Keep thou my feet;
I do not ask to see the distance scene
One step enough for me."[13]

What greater freedom could we have than to be able to go forward in our lives in confidence even though we don't have all the information. We can patiently and humbly wait on the Lord knowing His timing is perfect. With this kind of faith, we do not have to know the "why." We don't have to see the entire path before us. One step is enough for us. One step is enough for right now. Whatever words He gives us, as they come in His timing, are the "lamp at our feet" and the only illumination we need before us on the path.[14] Indeed, we become grateful simply because He is still leading us on.

Therefore, What?

As you examine ways you may have interpreted or given reason to revelation, consider first these questions:

- "Do I think I am supposed to interpret God's divine direction?"
- "Am I afraid to move without being able to see the whole path in front of me?"
- "Is the doubt or frustration I am feeling because I 'ran' with a revelation in the wrong direction?"
- "Have my interpretations of revelation caused me not to enjoy the process, or be unhappy with my life?"
- "Am I willing to allow the Lord to lead me, through His Spirit, not having to know beforehand what He is going to have me do?"

What's my reasoning? Next, reflect on a few of the promptings you may have received in the last little while. Write some of them down and, next to each one, write down what it seems the divine purpose of it was.

Next, reflect on whether God revealed His purposes to you at the time the prompting first came, later on, or maybe He still hasn't. Analyze and notice patterns of how the Lord reveals things to you and how often He might give you the "why." As we notice these patterns, we become more comfortable with the way the Lord directs our lives, fostering our faith in Him.

Also consider, have there been times that the Lord instructed you specifically to do something and, although you assumed it was for one reason, it ended up being for a different reason entirely? Have there been times you greatly limited the Lord because of your assumptions?

What kind of "why" are we asking? Another insight to consider is that there are different kinds of "why" questions. Elder Scott helps us see the difference. We can ask:

"Why do I have to do this?"
"Why am I supposed to quit my job?"
Or even "What is going to happen when I do this?"

Or we can instead ask:
"What am I to do?"
"What am I to learn from this experience?"
"What am I to change?"
"Who can I help?"
"How can I focus on the positive and remember how blessed I am during trials?"[15]

In addition, asking "why" can be beneficial if we are seeking doctrinal understanding. Remember, doctrine tells us why we do what we do. When we ask "why" as in "Why is the Lord asking me to pay tithing?" "Why are we counseled to read our scriptures?" etc., these kinds of questions can point us to find answers in the doctrine.

_____

_____

_____

[1] President Henry B. Eyring taught that "we almost always have more than one motive at a time. And some motives may be mixtures of what God wants as well as what we want. It is not easy to pull them apart." ("Gifts of the Spirit for Hard Times," *Ensign*, June 2007)

[2] "Apostles Talk about Reasons for Lifting Ban," *Daily Herald*, Provo, Utah (5 June 1988): 21 (Associated Press); reproduced with commentary in Dallin H. Oaks, *Life's Lessons Learned: Personal Reflections* (Salt Lake City, Utah: Deseret Book Co., 2011), p.68-69.

[3] This triangle can even include all our memories, the knowledge we gain and experiences we have throughout our lives, and even the things we learn from others. Regardless of how much we believe we see and understand, it is so miniscule in comparison to what God sees.

[4] D&C 38:2: "Thus saith the Lord your God, even Jesus Christ, the Great I AM, Alpha and Omega, the beginning and the end, the same which looked upon the wide expanse of eternity, and all the seraphic hosts of heaven, before the world was made; the same which knoweth all things, for [b]all things are present before mine eyes." D&C 130:6-7: "The angels do not reside on a planet like this earth; But they reside in the presence of God, on a globe like a sea of glass and fire, where all things for their glory are manifest, past, present, and future, and are continually before the Lord."

[5] The Prophet Joseph Smith taught, "The great Jehovah contemplated the whole of the events connected with the earth, pertaining to the plan of salvation, before it rolled into existence, or ever 'the morning stars sang together' for joy; the past, the present, and the future were and are, with Him, one eternal 'now;' He knew of the fall of Adam, the iniquities of the antediluvians, of the depth of iniquity that would be connected with the human family, their weakness and strength, their power and glory, apostasies, their crimes, their righteousness and iniquity; He comprehended the fall of man, and his redemption; He knew the plan of salvation and pointed it out; He was acquainted with the situation of all nations and with their destiny; He ordered all things according to the council of His own will; He knows the situation of both the living and the dead, and has made ample provision for their redemption, according to their several circumstances, and the laws of the kingdom of God, whether in this world, or in the world to come" (*Teachings of the Prophet Joseph Smith,* p. 220; *History of the Church,*4:597).

[6] Isaiah 55:8-9

[7] *The Mortal Messiah*, (1979-81), 1:238; emphasis added

[8] "Trust in the Lord," *Ensign*, November, 1995

[9] "God Moves in a Mysterious Way," *Hymns*, 285

[10] We are promised that when we sanctify ourselves, our minds becoming "single to God," our "whole bodies shall be filled with light, and there shall be no darkness" in us, and filled with this light we will be able to comprehend all things. But this will be done "in his own time, and in his own way, and according to his own will" (D&C 88:67-68)

[11] "Consider the Blessings," *Ensign*, November 2012

[12] 1 Nephi 4:6

[13] Hymns, 97

[14] Psalms 119:105

[15] Elder Richard G. Scott, "Trust in the Lord," *Ensign*, November 1995

HINDRANCE #9

Giving Reasons to Revelation Part II

At the same time that those amazing young women in D.C. were being taught about revelation and the workings of the Spirit by the Lord, I was being tutored, as well. For after we had been there a few years, I started getting the feeling that our time in Virginia might be coming to a close. Yet it was subtle enough that I didn't pay much attention to it.

However, the prompting got strong enough and came consistently enough that I finally mentioned something to Michelle about it. Interestingly, she had been having the same feeling. She described it as feeling "the winds of change beginning to blow." This was sometime in early March and, with her feelings to confirm mine, we concluded that we must be getting transferred with my job that summer. We began preparing for the move.

I must, at this point, share something with you about my personality. I have realized that I am a "finisher." When there is a task before me, my number one goal is to just get it done. This character trait is a great strength because I usually end up getting a lot of things done. (I love checklists.) But it can also be a weakness. (Just ask my family about our 14-hour road trips from California to Utah each summer. It takes too much time to stop for food or bathroom breaks. We've just got to "get it done!")

Well, for many years, I approached revelation much the same way: if I felt impressed to do something, I would just go do it. I wouldn't waste a lot of time wondering if I should or shouldn't (which maybe isn't a bad thing). However, I also wouldn't waste any time when it came to interpreting it. This was one of those times.

In my tendency to "run" to reason with that revelation, we immediately changed the agenda of our lives with six little children: no summer baseball, no commitments to help with the Ward party in August, no more additions to our food storage. Our plans to build a house were put on hold. Every week, we waited for the phone call to tell us we were moving.

Well, August rolled around and we were still firmly planted in Virginia. No phone call. No inkling, even, that something was going to happen. The impressions had pretty much stopped. In fact, another whole year went by and we were still living in Virginia. It was an incredibly confusing year.

It was then that I started learning some other facets of this concept of giving reasons to revelation that would change my understanding and experience with it. You see, when we give reasons to our revelations, it doesn't make us bad people; it simply makes the process of revelation much more difficult for us. In fact, in many ways our reasoning works against the process. That is usually because most of the time when we receive a divine instruction from our loving Heavenly Father it is usually a piece of a much larger picture.

Revelation is rarely singular. It is meant to be *continuous*.

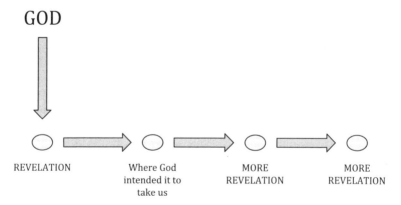

Elder Richard G. Scott taught, "Seldom does the whole answer to a decisively important matter or complex problem come all at once. More often, it comes a piece at a time, without the end in sight."[1]

Yes, sometimes there is "event" revelation, or a single instruction that solves an immediate problem or need: "Go visit your mom in the hospital." "Move your son out of the way." But those impressions almost seem to be the exception more than the rule.

You can see how this principle applied to my students: the revelation a young woman might get to move to D.C. isn't necessarily meant to be the first and last impression relating to that experience. Instead, it is meant perhaps to be the first part of a *series* of insights that will give her the experiences and stretching she needs while she is there.

Those wonderful sisters were not intentionally trying to take their revelation off course, but when they interpreted that revelation, they put themselves in the place where it was very difficult to receive further direction.

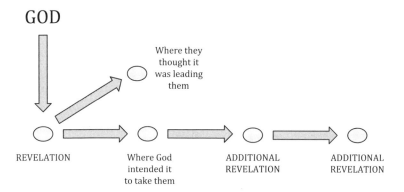

I've wondered: because they thought they already knew the reason for being there, were they even watching for the real reasons they were there? Were they able to learn what He intended them to learn? And was it difficult to hear any additional direction the Lord was trying to give them?

Is it any wonder, then, that they were struggling! They were stuck back on that first revelation and had removed themselves from the flow of learning and growth and experience God had lined out for them. When we take ourselves out of that current of divine help, revelation — and other fruits of the Spirit like peace, faith, joy, and patience — can be greatly obstructed, as well.[2]

In addition, I believe that because they knew they had received divine guidance initially to move to D.C., they mistakenly thought the direction they were headed was also divinely sanctioned. The only problem is that their direction had been influenced, or even completely changed, by their own added reasoning. Then, when things weren't turning out the way they had expected, their faith in their God, having been all tied up in the process, was severely tested.

You can also probably see by now how this principle also applied to our experience: the impressions that Michelle and I started getting in the beginning were just that — the *beginning* of a series of revelations that the Lord wanted to give us. However, we were too busy preparing for a move we had concluded was going to happen *that summer* to notice that.

I have wondered if that was why we felt like the heavens were closed for a while, because we were actually off in left field "leaning unto our own understanding" (Proverbs 3:5). We were stuck in one of those "dead ends" of our own reasoning. Spiritually, we just weren't where God needed us to be.

When we approach revelation with the understanding that it is often *continuous*, we prepare ourselves for a *journey* with revelation instead of a bunch of unrelated end destinations. We prepare our minds for the reality that there are still greater experiences and greater light in store for us. We realize that we are only going to get the pieces we need or can handle right now.

And sometimes that is simply because of the things we need to learn and experience along the way — which leads us to another great truth about revelation: revelation is usually continuous because *information often precedes revelation*. President Russell M. Nelson even taught, "Good revelation is based upon good information."[3]

If we find that we're struggling with a decision or cannot seem to discern the right choice, it could simply be because we don't have all the information yet. We must either pay the price to improve our understanding, or wait for future experiences to give us the vital information we need. We won't be able to know, or at least *understand,* what the Lord's will is in a situation until those requirements are met.

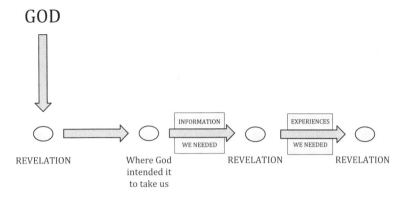

The Jaredites had an incredible experience with this principle when the Lord confounded the language of the people during the time of the Tower of Babel. God swore that all the people would be scattered across the face of the earth. However, He had mercy on the Brother of Jared and his people.[4]

He instructed them to gather all their flocks and seeds, and their families and friends, and go into the valley north of them. *"And there,"* He said, *"will I meet thee* and I will go before thee into a land which is choice above all the lands of the earth."[5]

And there I will meet you. In other words, "Just do what I have asked. You aren't going to know all the answers right now. Just go — go in faith with what you know right now. Have faith in the revelation you have already received."

So it is with us. "Have faith in the inspiration you felt when you weren't expecting it as you sat in the temple, or were commuting home, or stood washing the dishes, or were reading your scriptures. Have faith in the thoughts and feelings that came during church, while praying, or in a class that had nothing to do with what was going on in that class. Have faith and just go. Even if you are not done with school. Even if you don't have the perfect job yet. Even if it goes against online financial advice. Just go."

When we trust in this principle and receive the inspiration that we need for the moment, we can then move forward knowing that when we get to the next place prepared for us, *God will be there.*

He will be there in California or Mexico City or Washington D.C or Malawi. He will be there in the unfamiliar. He will be there with that new baby or in that new job or with that new calling. And until we get there, maybe the heavens seem a little silent because we just don't need to know anything else yet. Maybe we just need to experience the true nature of faith a little more, which is to believe in things not fully understood, and hope for things not seen.[6]

This principle has had a profound effect on many experiences throughout my life, especially in parenting and priesthood assignments. Often there have been decisions that needed to be made or counsel that needed to be given and I just didn't seem to be getting any real direction. And it has often simply been because some time needed to pass or more information was needed before that direction could come.

It also helped me understand why we were given promptings to move so long before the actual move. There were many things we needed to learn and many experiences we needed to have before we were ready for that move. In fact, we had the opportunity through our oldest son, Stephen, to share the gospel of Jesus Christ with an amazing woman and her two children who lived in our neighborhood. They are still dear friends today. Had we moved, I believe she would have still found her way to the Lord's church because of her goodness and pure heart, but we would have missed out on being a part of that miracle.

Our Father seems to use most, if not all, of our experiences to teach and change us. He seems to be much more concerned with our eternal growth and connection to Him than our having all the answers immediately in front of us.

A last lesson from our "moving from Virginia" experience came one night during the second summer of our waiting. I was struggling with the whole experience, trying to figure out how we both had gotten it so wrong, when this distinct impression came to my mind: "Just take this time to clean your life and ponder. Use this time to ask questions and prepare so that you can receive more."

It was a profound thought, and it involved "doing" something with revelation that I hadn't realized counted as "doing." Clean. Ponder. Ask. Prepare.

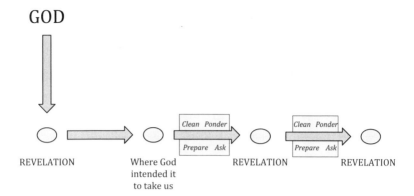

Those four simple words of counsel from this revelation changed the way I waited on the Lord from that point forward. Michelle and I consistently came back to these things as, together, we waited for answers and direction.

We learned that the impression to "clean" didn't necessarily just involve repentance. Yes, we must repent of sin so that we are worthy of revelation. However, we can also "clean" our lives by cleaning up our priorities, honestly examining our motives, or recognizing our limitations. We become more pure as we adjust our expectations, re-define the worldly definitions we might be applying to eternal things, or use Christ's Atonement to correct our false beliefs and perceptions.

The beauty of this truth is that we don't have to be perfect to receive revelation. Any kind of cleaning helps us become a little bit better, which qualifies us to receive a little bit more. As we become better people, we become less likely to taint the revelation He is sending to us and more prepared for when further direction comes.

We also learned how to ask the right questions. When the impression came to clean, prepare, ponder, and ask, at first we were a little confused about the "ask" part because we knew we had been asking a lot of questions. "When are we moving?" "Why are we moving?" "Where are we going?" "How is this all going to work out?" We realized, however, that those questions weren't necessarily what we should be asking.

Nephi didn't ask, "How am I going to do this?" when the Lord instructed him to build a ship. He asked, "Whither shall I go that I may find ore to molten, that I may make tools to construct the ship?" (1 Nephi 17:9). We learned to ask, "What do we need to learn right now — and where do we need to go to learn it?" "What do we need to focus on?" "Where does Thou need us to be?"

Over the years, I have also found myself being able to ponder much more often when I receive revelation. I've been able to receive an impression and just letting it settle in my mind and heart. Not running to meaning. Not even necessarily running to action just to feel like I am doing something, but just letting it settle — which is an incredibly amazing feat for this "finisher." The ways my mind has been enlightened and expanded with pure knowledge in the process has been incredible.

One friend of ours shared a similar experience:

> "One time, I felt a distinct impression I needed to have a difficult conversation with one of my adult daughters. I was not necessarily excited about it, not only because of some frustration I was feeling towards her, but also because those kinds of impressions cause me a lot stress. Usually, I immediately start worrying about what I'm going to say or how it's going to go. But this time, I decided to just ponder about it, pray about it, go to the temple about it, without worrying about what I was supposed to say, or even *when* I was supposed to say it. I also didn't worry about how she was going to react to it. No timeline. No expectations.
>
> "After a while, (a longer while than I anticipated, no less), the words and the right moment became very clear to me. My delivery wasn't the greatest, but it didn't matter. I was able to truly be an instrument. I will admit that I really wanted the Lord's assurance that our conversation was going to end well and that it wouldn't make my daughter angry at me. But there was no such reassurance. I came to not need it, however, the more confident I became in the message I was supposed to deliver. It was an incredibly different experience than I have had in the past."

I have discovered that the *timing* is just as, if not more, important as the message. And that is true not only with things we feel to share with others, but with things the Lord feels to share with us.

Lastly, we learned a little bit more about the preparation the Lord does in our waiting on Him, much like soil must be prepared before planting. If God gives us revelation before we are prepared for it, it can literally *damn* us — or hinder us from progressing. It holds us accountable for something we are not ready for or capable of yet. That is why His timing is so perfect. It's why His ways are so perfect. *He knows where we are at.* He knows if there are things we aren't quite ready to hear. He knows if there are still things we need to learn. He knows if we need to repent about something before we can accept a specific counsel. We do not always know those things.

Our experience with that move was a tutoring experience. Yes, it has taken us years to learn some things. (In fact, it was years before we actually moved — an absolutely necessary time of preparation for us for our family and the challenges that we would face in that new area.)

Yet, what an experience it has been. We have watched as the Lord, because of His wisdom and purposes, has weaved divine and customized lessons into our daily experiences, and especially our experiences with personal revelation.

As we commit to the journey of revelation, we prepare ourselves to receive help not only right now, but tomorrow and the next day and weeks down the road. "Line upon line." His divine sentences become part of a story we don't fully have yet. However, we trust anyway and direct our energies into finding peace in what has been given, regardless of how incomplete it may feel. Sometimes, when we are where we're supposed to be, doing what we're supposed to be doing, our loving Father gives us a whole paragraph at one time. It might even be an extraordinary peek into eternity that teaches us more in five seconds than we had learned all day. These visions are rare, but they are priceless. Someday, we will have the whole story and be able to tell and re-tell the narrative of how the Lord led us step by step to the conclusion.[7] And I'm only now really beginning to understand what a glorious story it will be.

Let us, then, enjoy the journey of revelation — delighting in each stop along the way, anxious to see where it will take us, but faithful enough to not have to know all the details right now.

Therefore, What?

Changing directions. One great truth in learning about the continuous aspect of revelation is that God will always give us opportunities to receive what He wants to give us. And if we get off track, through the power of Christ, we can always get back on track.

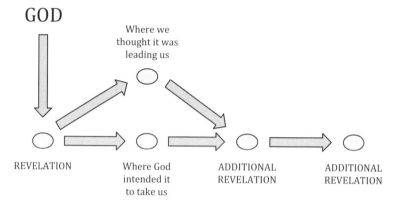

This seems to be what the Lord was doing with those unmarried sisters. He was trying to help them get back to the purity of their revelation and see what His purposes were in their lives. This is also what He has done in my life again and again over the years.

Thankfully, we really cannot mess this process up completely, despite our mistakes or misinterpretations. President Howard W. Hunter taught this truth that I believe applies here as well: "Please remember this one thing. If our lives and our faith are centered upon Jesus Christ and his restored gospel, nothing can ever go permanently wrong."[8]

What if God's answers don't end up being the answers we are looking for? We talked in Chapter 5 about the danger in wanting specific answers. However, there are times that God does give us a specific answer but it doesn't actually end up being the answer or solution to our situation — at least not in that moment, or at least not what we think the solution is supposed to be. When this happens, we often begin questioning the direction we've received.

For example, we may wonder:

- "Why did I feel impressed to apply for a different job if I wasn't even going to get it?"
- "Why did I feel really good about my daughter trying out for that ballet company if she wasn't going to make it?"
- "Why did I feel so good about dating this guy when it didn't end up working out?"
- "Why did I feel I was going to be called into the Young Women's presidency and I wasn't?"
- "Why did I feel to go down that street as a missionary and there was no one to teach?"
- "Why did I feel good about buying a specific home that came up for sale in my neighborhood (when I wasn't even really thinking about moving) only to get halfway through the process and someone else bought it instead?"
- "Why did I feel strongly that I was supposed to talk to my college-aged son about some of his choices when it just ended up causing such a huge argument he packed up his bags and moved out?"

Hopefully, the multitude of these questions helps us realize just how common this is. Every one of them is from someone I personally know who has asked those exact questions. We could each probably fill in the blank with our own experiences. Because we don't fully know God's purposes, we may not fully know why He does this. However, what I do know is that sometimes this is how He works.

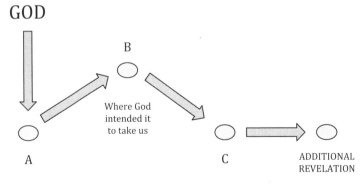

It seems sometimes He gives us those kinds of impressions to give us "practice" at following impressions. Other times, it seems to be because of things we need to learn from the experience, or things that need to be said regardless of how they will be received. Yet many times, there is really no logical explanation — at least not according to man's logic. God's higher purposes don't always fit into *man's* thinking and reasoning.

One of my students also added this insight:

"I have found that some of the clearest answers I have received have been revelations that were not the actual answer. What I mean by that is that they were revelations that led me from point A to point B, but point B wasn't the end destination. I have learned that often the times the Lord has been the most direct with me has been the times He needed me to move in a certain direction in order to find additional insight or have a certain experience that I needed, and then be led in sometimes a completely different direction the next time."

Discovering more how God works. Elder Holland's son, Matthew, shares an additional experience with this principle that helps us better understand it. Years ago, he and his dad were driving on a dirt road to find a lookout point over the Colorado River. With an old map in hand, they crossed miles of what looked like the exact same landscape.

As they reached their destination later that afternoon, they turned around to head home. The way looked the same, just the brownish tan of desert stretching for miles. It didn't take long before they reached a fork in the road. Elder Holland stopped the truck. He wasn't sure which way they had come. The sun was beginning to set in the distance.

Elder Holland and his son said a prayer, looked at each other, and both shared they felt they should "go left." Not ten minutes later, the trail came to a dead end. They turned around, headed back the other way and confidently made their way home. Then Matt asked the question, "Dad, why did we both feel like Heavenly Father told us to go down the road to the left when it was the wrong road?"

Elder Holland's response? "I've been thinking and silently praying about that same thing all the way home, because I really did feel a very distinct impression to take the road to the left. . . . The Lord has taught us an important lesson today. Because we were prompted to take the road to the left, we quickly discovered which one was the right one. . . . I was able to travel along its many unfamiliar twists and turnoffs perfectly confident I was headed in the right direction.

"If we had started on the right road, we might have driven for 30 minutes or so, become uneasy with the unfamiliar surroundings, and been tempted to turn back. If we had done that, we would have discovered the dead-end so late that it would have been too dark to find our way back in totally unfamiliar territory."[9]

Matthew Holland then adds, "Sometimes in response to prayers, the Lord may guide us down what *seems* to be the wrong road — or at least a road we don't understand — so, in due time, He can get us firmly and without question on the right road. Of course, He would never lead us down a path of sin, but He might lead us down a road of valuable experience. Sometimes in our journey through life we can get from point A to point C only by taking a short side road to point B."[10]

_____
_____
_____
_____
_____
_____
_____
_____
_____
_____
_____
_____
_____
_____
_____
_____
_____
_____
_____
_____

[1] "Learning to Recognize Answers to Prayer," *Ensign*, Nov 1989
[2] Galatians 5:22
[3] "Revelation for the Church, Revelation for Our Lives," *Ensign*, May 2018
[4] Ether 1:33
[5] vs. 42-43
[6] Alma 32:21; Ether 10:8
[7] Isaiah 28:10
[8] "'Fear Not, Little Flock,'" *Devotional and Fireside Speeches,* Provo: Brigham Young University Press, 1989, p. 112; the quote goes on to say, "On the other hand, if our lives are not centered on the Savior and his teachings, no other success can ever be permanently right."
[9] "Wrong Roads and Revelation," *New Era,* July 2005
[10] "Wrong Roads and Revelation," *New Era,* July 2005

HINDRANCE #10

Not Staying Present

Scenario #1: A single mother named Leanne was struggling to teach and discipline her willful teenage son. What first started as breaking curfew turned into refusing to go to Church, which turned into sluffing school. However, each time the behavior worsened, the mother disciplined less and less. But it was not because she didn't want to. It's just that she was struggling with some deep insecurity and overwhelming guilt.

Why? She had made some mistakes in parenting her son earlier in his life, and she believed his choices were her fault. She was so sure she had messed everything up with him, she couldn't figure out how to discipline him now. In Leanne's mind, his behavior was just an extension of her failure. She could not forgive herself for it nor forget about it, both of which were paralyzing her. Fear and frustration were part of her everyday interactions with him.

Scenario #2: Ben started feeling that he needed to switch to a different college in a different state. That school had a better program than the one he was currently attending and would allow him to better pursue his education. However, every time he thought about it, he would get a sick feeling inside. He was sure that meant he wasn't supposed to go.

The only problem? Any time Ben would even think about switching schools, his mind would become consumed with these thoughts: "Where am I going to live?" "How do I know things will work out?" "Will I find a job?" "What about all the transfer credits they won't take?" "Who will be my roommate?" "What if others think it's a stupid idea?" "What if I hate it?"

Have you ever found yourself, like Leanne, so paralyzed by something that has happened in the past that you feel unable to do something today? Have you, like Ben, worried so much about something that might happen in the future that you feel unable to make decisions today? Well, you're not alone — and it simply may indicate you are not staying present.

Lao Tzu, a Chinese philosopher, is quoted as saying:

> *If you are depressed, you are living in the past.*
> *If you are anxious, you are living in the future.*
> *If you are at peace, you are living in the present.*

We know what it feels like when we dwell on the past — holding on to mistakes we've made or repeatedly going back to the disappointments in our lives. We feel helpless. We feel hopeless. We feel depressed. And if we stay there long enough, we *get stuck* somewhere back in that past. We are trapped by something we can no longer do anything about.

We also know what it feels like to worry about what might happen somewhere down the road. We feel anxious. We panic. We look to some future event when we will finally be happy or successful. We just want today to get over with already. In the process, we lose sight of the people and circumstances that need our attention right in front of us. Today becomes a blur because we are actually *living* in the future.

None of those feelings and experiences seem peaceful in any way. And there's a reason for that. There's a reason, as Lao stated, that peace cannot be found by living in the past or future. And, in many ways, it has to do with revelation.

In C.S. Lewis' *The Screwtape Letters*, we read about a head devil named Screwtape who is training Wormwood, his apprentice, on how to lead humans away from their Enemy (or God). At one point, Screwtape tells Wormwood, "The humans live in time but the Enemy destines them for eternity. He therefore, I believe, wants them to attend chiefly to two things, to eternity itself, and to that point of time which they call the Present. *For the Present is the point at which time touches eternity. . . .*

"He would therefore have them continually concerned either with eternity (which means being concerned with Himself) or the Present. . . . Our business is to get them away from the eternal and from the Present . . . . We sometimes tempt a human to live in the past . . . . He (God) does not want men to give the Future their hearts . . . . We do . . . we want a man hag-ridden by the Future."[1]

What an incredible concept. *The Present is where time touches eternity.* If that is true, it seems, the present would also be the place where God is. As I've pondered on this idea over the years, I've begun to notice some clues that this might be so. For example, notice how often the Lord calls Himself "I Am." In the Doctrine and Covenants, He declared, "Hearken and listen to the voice of him who is from all eternity to all eternity, *the Great I AM*" (D&C 39:1, emphasis added; 29:1).

Another time He introduces Himself as "the Great I AM, Alpha and Omega, the beginning and the end, the same which looked upon the wide expanse of eternity . . . the same which knoweth all things, *for all things are present before mine eyes*" (D&C 38:1-2, emphasis added). He said to his apostles, "*I am* the way, the truth, and the life" (John 14:6). Even the statements "I am the first and the last" and "I am he who liveth" denote an eternal presence *in the present* (D&C 110:4; 1 Nephi 20:12).

I even think about the time when God came to Moses in the burning bush. The children of Israel had been in bondage to the Egyptians for about 400 years, and God called the young Moses to deliver them from their bondage. Moses is unsure and afraid. The Lord tells him he is to go before Pharaoh to bring His people out of Egypt. Moses wonders why the Lord is asking him, of all people, to do this. Yet, the Lord reassures him, "I will be with thee" (Exodus 3:12).

Moses then asks, "When I come unto the children of Israel, and shall say unto them, The God of your fathers hath sent me unto you; and they shall say to me, What is his name? what shall I say unto them?" (v. 13). And then God answers Moses with this: "I AM THAT I AM. . . . Thus shalt thou say unto the children of Israel, I AM hath sent me unto you. . . . This is my name for ever . . ." (vs. 14-15).

Notice there is no past or future tense in these phrases. Notice there doesn't seem to be any past or future even when He is talking about eternity. There are dozens more declarations like these in the scriptures. God's eternal existence seems to always be in the present and, thus, it seems, this is the place where we can connect with Him.[2] And if the present is where we connect with eternity and where we connect with God, it would seem, then, that the present is where we can receive messages from God. It would seem the present is where revelation flows. Thus, it is the place where peace — and every other fruit of His Spirit — can be found.

And so, simply put, another way we can hinder revelation in our lives is by not staying present. We hinder the ability for God to communicate with us when we are not where He is. It becomes very difficult to receive or act on revelation when we are not where revelation flows. And the adversary, as Lewis so brilliantly explained, will do whatever he has to, *and in whatever way he has to,* to cause us to live in some other time and place than where God is. Satan wants us to disconnect from the present and hinder the flow of that communication in our lives.

Think of the first scenario. Leanne struggled being divinely guided in behalf of her son because she was so caught up in what had happened in the past. She couldn't see clearly what actions she should take today because her vision was muddled by the things she couldn't forgive herself for. She was not where revelation — and healing and forgiveness and wisdom — could flow.

Another young man I knew struggled to find the peace, guidance, and healing he desperately needed in his life because he so often dwelt on the damaging things that had happened to him when he was young. In his mind, he was not worth anything to anyone.

Now, I know somewhat of the depth of his pain and the challenging experiences he had endured. However, I also know that he was an amazing young man with great potential who truly desired divine help and healing. He was just putting himself in a place where that divine help and healing was much more difficult to find.

When we live in the past, it inevitably causes frustrating, discouraging, and depressing feelings. *Frustration, discouragement, and depression all hinder revelation.* Sharon, a middle-aged mother, shared with me, "I sat in testimony meeting one Sunday filled with hopelessness about something I had discovered had happened to one of our children years before. It was an overwhelming trial that I wasn't handling very well and couldn't stop dwelling on. The thought came to me, 'Even if the Spirit did prompt me to bear my testimony, it wouldn't matter. I wouldn't be able to follow it.' It seemed it wouldn't matter what the Spirit told me to do right then, I probably wouldn't have been able to do it. Even if something someone said in their testimony was meant specifically for me and what I was struggling with, I'm not sure I would have been able to hear it. My mind was just too consumed with those negative thoughts from something in the past."[3]

Elder Jeffrey R. Holland counseled, "I plead with you not to dwell on days now gone nor to yearn vainly for yesterdays. . . . The past is to be learned from but not lived in."[4] It's not that we shouldn't ever think about the past. We must deal with the past. We can't just sweep it under a rug and foolishly think that it won't come creeping back out someday. However, dealing with the past is not dwelling on it, blaming it, or allowing it to consume us today. *Dealing with the past is not living in it.*

We can also hinder revelation when we live in the future. As Ben was trying to figure out if he should switch to a different college, he was consumed with every detail of what *could* go wrong if he did. He may have felt sick each time he thought about moving, but those feelings may not have been from the Spirit. They could have been from his own worry and fear of the future.

I've watched young people try to move forward in relationships. Often, they pray for guidance with questions like: "What if it doesn't work out?" "What if I found out something about her that I don't like?" What if we fight? "How can I get a guarantee that he is the 'right' one?" They are so stressed about how a relationship is *going to turn out*, they disconnect from that relationship — *and from revelation* — in the moment.

Missionaries can worry so much about getting someone to commit to baptism, they can lose inspiration about what that person needs today to take that next step. We can allow fears about where the economy is going to skew our ability to make crucial decisions right now. Parents can worry so much about what their kids *might* do in a given situation, they "feel impressed" to never let them go anywhere. Or they see a negative behavior going on in their lives today and envision a delinquent five years down the road.

Regardless of the situation, it is very difficult to receive revelation when we are hag-ridden by worries for the future. In fact, it often comes to a screeching halt. Then, we mistakenly wonder why heaven isn't helping us in some of our most important decisions.

It's not that we shouldn't think about the future. However, "dwelling on" is not the same as "dealing with." We must invest in relationships now in order to have strong relationships later. We should plan for our children's education. We must save money for future medical expenses. We must anticipate future events. The Lord sometimes even specifically has us prepare for things in the future. However, that preparation is done by focusing on what needs to be taken care of in the present.

We find this principle in an incredible miracle from the Israelites' 40-year journey through the wilderness. Shortly after they had walked through the Red Sea on dry ground, the children of Israel quickly forgot the mercy and deliverance of the Lord. They began to grumble about the lack of food.[5] Instead of showing gratitude for their freedom or exercising faith that He would provide for them again, they complained. They told Moses they would have rather died as slaves to the Egyptians, sitting by the fleshpots, than wander around in the wilderness dying from hunger.[6]

Now, we know that their nomadic lifestyle largely prevented this multitude of Israelites from hunting game or growing sufficient crops to feed everyone. Food was going to be an ever-present need during their exodus. Moses knew that. The Lord knew that. Yet it seems God also knew their wandering, fickle hearts needed some refining.

And so, incredibly — even in their murmuring, even in their lack of trust in Him — He chose to rain down "bread from heaven" every day except the Sabbath to feed them. They called it *manna* (which literally meant "What is this?") and it appeared on the ground day after day, six mornings of the week . . . *for forty years*.[7]

Elder D. Todd Christofferson explained, "By providing a daily sustenance, one day at a time, Jehovah was trying to teach faith to a nation that over a period of some 400 years had lost much of the faith of their fathers. He was teaching them to trust Him, to 'look unto [Him] in every thought; doubt not, fear not' (D&C 6:36). He was providing enough for one day at a time. . . . In essence, the children of Israel had to walk with Him today and trust that He would grant a sufficient amount of food for the next day *on* the next day, and so on. In that way, He could never be too far from their minds and hearts. . . ."[8]

For the Israelites, their God was found in the present. And because He is the same "yesterday, today, and forever" (Mormon 9:9), our God is also found in the present. His "manna" — His guidance, His comfort, His revelation, and anything else He is raining down from heaven — is found in the present. We may not always recognize what He is doing for us. Yet, we still must, like the Israelites, "look to God each day for the bread — the help and sustenance — we require in that particular day."[9] As tempting as it may be to run ahead with our needs or try to find answers today for future problems, each day we need to go to Him for the help or guidance for that day. As we do this, we keep ourselves present.

I was inspired years ago by the courageous story of Malala Yousafzai, the young girl from Pakistan who was shot by the Taliban for trying to attend school in 2012. After receiving fairly primitive medical treatment in a village hospital, she was flown to a military hospital. A surgeon there was impressed to remove not only the bullet in her brain, but also part of her skull to relieve pressure on her brain.

Miraculously, a few hours later, two British doctors, who were in Pakistan setting up a liver transplant program, just happened to be in the same hospital where she was recovering. They were specifically trained in procedures to treat her injury, knew what additional care she would need to survive, and had connections in the United Kingdom to get her that care. As her family marveled at all the right people being in all the right places, one of these British physicians, Dr. Javid Kayani, simply testified, "It is my belief God sends the solution first and the problem later."[10]

We may not always realize it, but divine solutions are found in the present. Sometimes they are in the form of people or circumstances prepared long before they are needed. Sometimes they are insights or impressions received long before we understand what they fully mean. Some solutions remain completely unknown to us until the very moment they are needed. Regardless, God often prepares solutions and answers and deliverance for us that can only be received when we are where He is — following His guidance in the moment, regardless if we fully understand why.

I have found that means sometimes His guidance won't make sense in the present. For example, it didn't make sense for the widow of Zaraphath to give her last meal to the prophet Elisha. Nephi probably wondered why he was supposed to painstakingly duplicate some of his father's record. We have so many examples where the Lord's commands didn't make sense in the moment. But remember the diagram with the triangles? Remember how much we, as mortals, can really see? These things make sense to God because of what He can see down the road, outside of the parameters of our triangle. He truly can see down the road in each one of our lives.

Recently, I had an interesting experience that gives us yet another way of looking at this principle. Often, if we are focusing too much on either the past or the future we will struggle *receiving* revelation. However, I also know that focusing too much on the past or the future interferes with revelation *we have already received.*

Michelle and I had to make a decision for our family over a weekend that involved a lot of future events — something that could be a great blessing to our family but that also involved some risks and some unknowns. As we ran numbers, looked at all of our options, tried to become as informed as possible about the situation, and sought the

Lord's guidance, we felt good about it and felt to move forward with the decision.

That is . . . at least, for a few hours. And then we would start to stress again. We would run numbers again, talk it over, look at all the options again, and discern how we felt, to then find assurance that it felt right . . . at least for a little bit.

After doing this several times over that weekend, we couldn't figure out what was going on. And then the lightbulb turned on! We were not staying present with the revelation. We would feel really good about the decision in the moment, in the present. But, inadvertently, one or both of us, would begin worrying about the future, the unknowns, the risks, all the things that could go wrong, etc. As soon as we started thinking in the future, we would begin to stress and worry about it. So, we decided to stay present and pay attention to what we were feeling in the present, moving forward with our decision, but only as fast as the present was moving forward.

President Brigham Young once shared the following in a sermon he delivered many years before the Salt Lake Temple was completed:

> "Some will inquire, 'Do you suppose we shall finish this Temple, brother Brigham?' I have had such questions put to me already. My answer is, I do not know, and I do not care anymore about it than I should if my body was dead and in the grave, and my spirit in Paradise. I never cared but for one thing, and that is, simply to know *that I am now right before my Father in Heaven*. If I am this moment, this day, doing the things God requires of my hands, and precisely where my Father in Heaven wants me to be, I care no more about tomorrow than though it would never come. I do not know where I shall be tomorrow, nor when this Temple will be done — I know no more about it than you do.... This I do know — there should be a Temple built here. I do know it is the duty of this people to commence to build a Temple."[11]

What amazing, faithful words. Yet, let's just think about Brigham's situation for a minute. He was given a divine directive from God to build a temple. Thousands of Saints worked for thousands of hours, years upon end, to help build it. At one point, the foundation stones, which took almost a decade to construct and lay, had to be torn out and replaced because they were unstable.

Every day, Brigham was faced with something that was taking much longer to finish than anyone expected. He could have focused on the past, and all the time, energy and money that had been invested in building that temple. So much sacrifice had already been made. He could have constantly worried about when it was going to be done, and when he could take that finished assignment to the Lord. Surely, he wanted that temple completed just as badly as anyone. Surely, he understood how much the Saints needed and desired to have a temple to worship in.

But he didn't worry about that. That was the Lord's concern. He focused on each day and his ability to, in each moment, do the things He was requiring of him. Brigham made himself be where God needed Him to be. These are amazing, faithful words. Nevertheless, they were spoken by a man who *knew*, probably more than many of us, what it felt like to wait on the Lord in the present.

The more time we spend in the present, the more we can see "things as they really are" and see as God sees (Jacob 4:13). We will realize, for example, that, God doesn't seem to look at us through the lens of the past. Otherwise, He probably never would have called Saul on the road to Damascus. He is focused on this point in our eternity. Because of Christ's Atonement, our yesterdays don't have to hold tomorrow hostage.[12]

In fact, when you look closely, the Atonement of Jesus Christ is a doctrine *of the present*. It may have the power to heal the wounds and fix the mistakes of the past, but that healing is done in the present. He heals in the present so that we can live in the present. Christ's Atonement also gives us the courage and faith we need to serve, love, repent, and persevere because it gives us hope — which is a principle of the present that applies to the future. Through Him, we can have hope today, right now, that things will eventually work out and that we will eventually become better.

Indeed, it seems all the principles of the gospel function in and keep us focused on the present. Patience, faith, forgiveness, trust — they all involve things that might be in the past or the future, but they require us to stay present in order to live by them.

There are things the Lord needs us to learn, progress we need to make, things we need to experience deeply and completely . . . today. There are relationships He needs us to build, people He needs us to lift, eyes that need to be met, hands that need to held . . . today. There may be things that need to be healed from the past. There may be decisions that must be made for the future. Even so, the only place that He can give us something that we need for the past or the future is right here, right now, where we are physically and literally at.

Elder Christofferson further counseled, "We . . . must learn to trust in our God and look to Him in every thought. We must not look back on what has happened, but trust that what we receive today can take care of the past. We must walk with Him today on perilous paths and trust in His promise that He will grant today a sufficient amount of what we need for tomorrow when tomorrow comes."

And then he promised this: "The Spirit can guide us when to look ahead and when we should just deal with this one day, with this one moment."[13] I believe the Spirit can also guide us when we need to look behind us to figure out something in the past. If every day we diligently pray to have this wisdom, we can stay present.[14]

Peace is found in the present. Healing is found in the present. Solutions are found in the present. Revelation is found in the present. Eternity is found in the present. Because God is found in the present.

So, let's stay present.

Therefore, What?

As you consider ways your focus on the past or the future is hindering revelation in your life, also consider these additional insights:

Know that it won't be easy at first. You may already know this, but it isn't necessarily easy to stay present. The nature of this world we live in and the adversary's relentless influence on it make sure of that. And just as the pull of the building drew multitudes away from the straight and narrow path, the past and the future have their own pull in our lives.

Do you find that you struggle with regret, guilt, or disappointment because of something in your past? Do you struggle with fear, anxiety, and worry about the future? If your focus is on the present, does it involve someone else's "shiny and perfect present" posted on social media — and how much *your* "present" stinks by comparison?

Staying present is a mindset that we often have to train ourselves to use. It isn't always going to come naturally. Thus, I don't believe we can change or strengthen this mindset without some divine help, no matter how determined we are.

I have found that the more we know God and trust in Him, the easier it is to do. After all, we must hand our past and future to Him; we must place into His hands all our pain or regret and all our fear or anxiety. We are not going to be as apt to do that if we don't know Him very well. Thus, sometimes this "handing over" must be done step by step, issue by issue, placing things on the altar one at a time.

Even when we are well aware of this concept, it is so easy to fall back into familiar patterns. I know there are times when I start to express concern to Michelle about something down the road and she has to remind me, "Stay present, Stephen. Just stay present." Other times she talks with me about mistakes she's made or something hurtful someone said to her and I remind her, "Stay present. Just focus on what is the most important thing you need to do today."

If you want to know how you are doing in this area, take stock of where your focus is right now in your family, in your extended family, in your work life, in your discipleship. How "in tune" are you to what you have power over today?

Know there's more than one way to stay present. I have also found that there are also ways to be present in the moment, but *not necessarily present*. Perhaps we are not all caught up in what happened yesterday. Or we aren't focused on what needs to happen tomorrow. We are "present" in time *but our hearts and minds are elsewhere*. Maybe they're at work. Or they're at school. Maybe we're "present" in a classroom but looking at Instagram, "present" in Sunday School but worried more about our lesson the next hour. Maybe we're "present" at work, but "at" a shopping website.

We can be "present" with our families, but, in reality, we are not. We are on our phones playing games or focusing on what other people are doing and saying and feeling instead of what our family is doing and saying and feeling. When we aren't present as a neighbor or friend, we may miss specific guidance God is giving us for them. When we aren't present on a date, we may miss something we're meant to learn from that person.

One stay-at-home mother shared with me that it is also an ever-present battle to "stay-at-home" with her mind and heart; online distractions, social pressures, and "small" commitments often pull her away throughout the day from the needs of her family. Now more than ever before, we can be present but distant at the same time. Yet, it is a great challenge that we can overcome the more we are aware of it and the more we focus on the eternal things that are ever present before us.

[1] *The Screwtape Letters*, C.S. Lewis, pp. 75-77, emphasis added

[2] Elder Neal A. Maxwell even uses a phrase "the holy present" in one of his talks, a concept that I believe could be studied further. ("Content with the Things Allotted unto Us," *Ensign*, May 2000)

[3] Elder Richard G. Scott taught that "the inspiring influence of the Holy Spirit can be overcome or masked by strong emotions, such as anger, hate, passion, fear, or pride. When such influences are present, it is like trying to savor the delicate flavor of a grape while eating a jalapeño pepper. Both flavors are present, but one completely overpowers the other. In like manner, strong emotions overcome the delicate promptings of the Holy Spirit. ("To Acquire Spiritual Guidance," *Ensign*, November 2009)

[4] "The Best is Yet to Be," *Ensign*, January 2010, from an address given at a BYU Devotional on January 13, 2009; "I plead with you not to dwell on days now gone nor to yearn vainly for yesterdays, however good those yesterdays may have been. The past is to be learned from but not lived in. We look back to claim the embers from glowing experiences but not the ashes. And when we have learned what we need to learn and have brought with us the best that we have experienced, then we look ahead and remember that *faith is always pointed toward the future.* Faith always has to do with blessings and truths and events that will *yet* be efficacious in our lives."; Elder Russell M. Nelson also taught, "I learned years ago from President N. Eldon Tanner never to look back. He taught me not to look through the 'retrospectroscope' and agonize over what I might have done differently. So I don't relive the past. Each hour had its opportunity, and I either did a good job or I fumbled the ball. I walk away from the past knowing I gave it the best I had." ("Elder Russell M. Nelson," by Marvin K. Gardner, *Ensign*, June 1984)

[5] Exodus 14:16; Joshua 3:17

[6] Exodus 16:3

[7] vs. 4, 6, 15

[8] "Give Us This Day Our Daily Bread," CES Fireside for Young Adults, January 9, 2011, Brigham Young University

[9] Elder D. Todd Christofferson, "Give Us This Day Our Daily Bread," CES Fireside for Young Adults, January 9, 2011, Brigham Young University

[10] "It is my belief that God sends the solution first and the problem later." Malala Yousafzai, *I Am Malala: The Girl Who Stood Up for Education and Was Shot by the Taliban,* Thorndike Press, 2018, p.161

[11] Brigham Young, *Journal of Discourse* Vol. 1, 22, emphasis added

[12] "Hope Through the Atonement," *Ensign*, November 1998

[13] "Give Us This Day Our Daily Bread," (CES Fireside for Young Adults, January 9, 2011, Brigham Young University); emphasis added

[14] Matthew 6:9-11

CONCLUSION

"Placing Our Lives in His Hands"

To conclude, I would like to share the story of a dear friend of ours names Becky:

"It was June 18th and just an all-around beautiful day. Being the Monday after Father's Day and the day before girl's camp, life was good and we were busy getting ready for all that was going on in our lives. Harrison, our teenage son, and I had made a dinner from a cookbook we had bought that day which Scott and the kids gave a 'thumbs up' to.

"The table was cleared by all. Scott and Harrison decided to go and take Scott's new bike from Father's Day for a ride, while my daughter and I were going to run to the store for some last-minute gifts for camp. Our younger son decided to go on a walk with my sister who lives nearby. We all said our goodbyes and I got my usual kiss and 'I love you.'

"I guess Scott and Harrison took off at quite a speed, which surprised Harrison as his dad was really not in great shape for a lengthy ride. Harrison realized he had forgotten his phone, and felt to go back to get it and then tried to catch up with his dad.

"About a half an hour later, we were on our way home from the store, and I missed a call on my cell phone. A few minutes later, my phone rang again. Someone on the other end said, 'Come quickly. There has been an accident . . . your son needs you.' All I could think of was Scott must have fallen or something and Harrison couldn't help him. Scott was a big man and Harrison was still young.

"I could never have imagined what was around the curve in the road . . . fire trucks . . . police cars . . . a rolled car . . . and a crumpled bike. My husband had been hit by a drunk driver. We lost him that night.

171

"There are things I know are true. One is that the things we learn in our youth will carry us when we are older. My favorite scripture has always been, 'Be still and know that I am God.'[1] I truly learned that night that if we are 'still,' we will be blessed with a peace that passes understanding. That is just one of the many gifts we were given. The power of the priesthood is so strong. Blessings from those holding authority gave us enough peace to be 'still'.

"As we went through the next few weeks trying to figure out our new normal, I learned to just breathe, to just hang on, to let go . . . and let Heavenly Father carry us. We also learned that service is a gift. We have always been taught that and it is true. We learned to do things for others when things got rough.

"I later learned that Harrison had tried to catch up with his dad, but couldn't seem to no matter how fast he peddled. I believe by then Scott knew he had to stay far away from Harrison so that he could protect him from the other side. But it was still very difficult for Harrison to accept.

"One day, he said to me that he never wanted to go near the place where his father had been killed. But I knew that Scott would never want any of us to use his death as a reason to fail. I asked him to come with me for a minute. We then proceeded to drive straight to the accident site. 'Harrison, this place is a sacred place,' I said. 'When heaven and earth collided that day in June, the veil became very thin. It is a place to never be afraid of. We need to visit here often.'

"I discovered from this tragic experience that having the agency to choose what to do with what happened was a great gift. It truly was a beautiful day that day, it was just a horrible accident. We can't change what happened, but out of something so tragic we have been blessed in so very many ways.

"Before this happened, I believed that death is not the end, that we are not alone. I had faith that we don't have to carry our trials by ourselves and that the sun will shine tomorrow. But Scott's death has been a sacred experience for me and losing him has changed my *faith* to *knowledge*. You see, Heavenly Father has a perfect plan if we will allow it to unfold in our lives. Living what we know to be true and placing our lives in His hands, He will guide us."[2]

I felt to conclude with Becky's story because it seemed to perfectly encapsulate everything we have been talking about here. Even in her tragedy — indeed, even when everything before her was nothing like what she had envisioned her life would look like — she trusted in God. Because she trusted Him, she looked to Him, relied on Him, and stayed connected to Him.

Becky "stayed present" in her circumstances, not looking back at what could have been done differently nor looking ahead to all the many things in her life that would never be the same. She didn't "box the Lord in" by limiting Him or refusing to consider the impression that the very thing Harrison needed was to go straight to the accident site. She didn't "cast her eyes about" to the horizontal around her to figure out how to adjust to their new normal. Nor did she follow worldly advice that revenge would solve her problems.

She didn't allow her mind to become encumbered by everything that was happening, but instead chose to "be still" in each moment; she chose to stay present! It seems she also didn't have a "recipe" for her life, and so she wasn't paralyzed by thoughts like "This wasn't supposed to happen to me" or "I can never be happy again." She had the wisdom and knowledge to trust in God's "perfect plan" for her life even if it wasn't *her* idea of a perfect plan.

Because of these choices, we can see how God was able to pour down knowledge from heaven upon her and her family. Look at all the incredible things He was able to reveal to her.

Becky would be the first to admit that she isn't perfect and that she didn't do everything right during that time of healing and adjustment. Still, she did a remarkable job of opening — and keeping open — the doors and windows in her life so that the warmth, light, and healing power of God could pour in. He was able to teach her. He was able to show her great things. He was able to reveal His mind and will to her. It seems He was also able to begin the process of strengthening and healing her and her children, filling them with His peace and power.

And I know that Becky's story could be so many of our stories.

When you think about it, one of the greatest tests of our mortal experience is whether or not we will trust our God. Trust is the underlying principle of obedience and faith and patience and even peace. It is something we have to choose to do every day and in every circumstance.

At another point in their journey, when the children of Israel were struggling (again!) to be grateful and humble in their trying circumstances, "the Lord sent fiery serpents among the people, and they bit the people; and much people of Israel died."[3] Realizing their responsibility in that trial, the Israelites pled with Moses to ask the Lord if He would take the snakes away. Moses asked. But the Lord responded with an unexpected solution.

He instructed Moses to make a serpent of brass, put it on a stick, and hold it up. Moses then told the people that if they would look up to that brazen serpent, they would live. Hundreds of poisonous snakes were slithering at their feet and biting them; people standing next to them were getting bit, possibly screaming with pain; some of their loved ones and children were probably dying. Yet God was asking them to take their attention off all that . . . and look *up*.

It seems He is still asking that of us today. He is asking us to take our eyes off our worries and our wounds. He is asking us to give up our world of unrealistic expectations and meticulous plans and mortal reasons. He is asking us to trust in Him by looking to Him for answers and reassurance and healing.

Trust is one of the most important underlying principles of revelation. If we don't genuinely trust our Heavenly Father, why would we pray to Him? Why would we ask Him what to do? Why would we value His opinion? If we do actually pray but don't really trust Him, how likely will we be to believe what He says? How likely will we be to follow His guidance?

Trust in the Lord is also what allows us to dismantle our boxes and accept His answers without parameters. It allows us to set aside our expectations or our need to be in control of everything and accept His plan. It is what gives us the ability to look up when everything around us is insisting we "cast our eyes about."

Trusting God allows us to accept an answer without having to know why it's the answer. It uncovers truth and dispels doubt and fear. When we trust Him, we don't have to rely on others revelation for we know He will guide us individually for our needs. When we trust Him, we are not paralyzed by the past or worried about the future.

Just like with any relationship here on earth, the more we come to know God, the more we will trust Him. Indeed, the Prophet Joseph Smith taught that in order for any of us to really be able to believe in and trust in Him, we must have a correct idea of His character, perfections, and attributes; in other words, we must come to know who He really is.[4]

We come to know these things about our God just as we would come to know these things about any person in our lives — we learn about Him, talk to Him, listen to Him, and watch Him as He works in our lives and in other's lives.

As we do these things, we will find continual evidence of how much He loves His children and how He has not left us to navigate this world alone. He has provided us with counsel, direction, and wisdom beyond our own, and He always will.

When the Lord commanded Lehi that he should take his family and set out into the wilderness, the very next morning Lehi walked out of his tent and found the Liahona — a *guide* that could tell them where they needed to go as they worked their way through that wilderness.[5]

However, they had to learn how to use it. When they were diligent and committed, it showed them a direct route to their next destination. When they were lazy or indifferent to it, it stopped working, and they would wander around through the wilderness suffering unnecessarily because of the delay.[6] Throughout their journey, they had experience after experience that helped them understand how to use it.

We, too, have been given a "Liahona" that we have to learn how to use. We have to learn how this personal guidance from the Lord works. It is a process that involves patience, effort, time, and experience. Every single thing we learn about revelation blesses us. Every time we practice it, we become better at it. Every false belief that is removed about revelation will clear up our minds and clear out space so that divine impressions can come. Every time we apply a true principle of revelation in our lives, it increases the light in our lives. It is a lifelong pursuit that we get better at the more we use it.

I love what this sister shared about this process: "There is more to this process of understanding revelation than simply figuring out the right answers. *Heavenly Father wants us to know Him.* We come to know Him by seeking His voice among all the voices clamoring for our attention and then by choosing that voice above all others. I have made many mistakes in trying to learn discernment. Mistakes occur in the course of practicing a skill; they show us our weaknesses so we can be humble and teachable.

"This is a lifelong endeavor, but that does not mean we have to wait an entire lifetime to succeed. If we are prepared when we knock, the door will be opened. I believe our Heavenly Father is so desirous of having us return to His presence that He will make use of every opportunity we give Him — 'even if [we] can no more than desire' to receive His direction (Alma 32:27). It generally begins with small and simple things."[7]

This lifelong endeavor of understanding, receiving and acting on personal revelation is a glorious one. It involves discovering ways revelation is working, ways that power and knowledge and peace are pouring down from heaven into our lives. It is about finding answers and knowing what those answers look like and feel like. It is finding healing because those answers haven't been deflected or distorted by untruth.

It also involves understanding better some of the obvious and less obvious ways we can hinder that revelation in our lives. It involves starting on a journey of unraveling any confusion or doubt or frustration we may have had with the process.

President Brigham Young once observed (and Elder Neal A. Maxwell and others later emphasized) that although we have been given the Spirit of the Lord to guide and direct us and even reveal the Lord's will to us, we can sadly "live far beneath our privileges."[8]

Oh, may we not live beneath our privileges! Let us rise up to those privileges! Let us recognize and remove the adversary's interference in our lives. Let us discover the things *we* do to interfere with it ourselves. Let us turn to our Savior, Jesus Christ, for His healing, His correcting, His refining, His miraculous transforming power so that He can prepare us and purify us and place us in the way of heaven's light.

Alma taught that when Lehi and his family were truly exercising faith, they were miraculously guided by the power of God "day by day" by the Liahona (Alma 37:40). Nephi and Lehi, the sons of Helaman, were even "having many revelations daily" as they worked to bring peace and the words of the Lord to their people (Helaman 11:23). And Sister Julie B. Beck testified that, in these latter days, "revelation can come *hour by hour* and *moment by moment* as we do the right things."[9]

Oh, may we have many revelations daily, even hour by hour and moment by moment!

The Lord promises us, "If thou shalt ask, thou shalt receive revelation upon revelation, knowledge upon knowledge, that thou mayest know the mysteries and peaceable things — that which bringeth joy, that which bringeth life eternal (D&C 61:42)." If we ask, if we seek, if we "feast" as Nephi taught and esteem the words that come from God's mouth more than food as Job did, we can know what is unknown to us right now.[10]

Heavenly Father truly does have a perfect plan for each one of us that will not only bring us joy, but eternal life. He wants to reveal it to us — day by day, piece by piece — if we will allow it to come pouring into our lives. The more revelation is a part of our daily, even hourly, thought process, the more we are thinking and feeling as God would think and feel — all a part of the process of becoming more like Him.

As we remove the barriers that are blocking the doors and covering up the windows to God's light in our lives, and place our lives — and our worldly desires, our limitations, our false beliefs, our expectations, our recipes, our interpretations, our need for specifics, our encumbered minds, our reliance on others' guidance, or our worries about the past and the future — in His hands, He will freely and willingly guide us.

Oh, may we have the courage and faith and trust and wisdom to place our lives in His hands so that we may be guided by Him.

_____

[1] D&C 101:16

[2] Story used by permission, Rebecca Snider Osman, 2011

[3] Numbers 21:6

[4] Lectures on Faith, Lecture 3 "The Character of God"

[5] 1 Nephi 16: 9-11; Alma 37:39

[6] Alma 37:39-42

[7] Personal story by Kiersten Olson, "Questions and Answers," *Ensign,* March 2007

[8] *Discourses of Brigham Young,* sel. and arr. by John A. Widtsoe, Salt Lake City: Deseret Book Co., 1973, p. 32; The Promise of Discipleship. Salt Lake City, UT: Deseret Book; *Deseret News Semi-Weekly,* 3 Dec. 1867, 2

[9] "And Upon the Handmaids of the Lord," *Ensign*, May 2010; "Stand as True Millennials," *Ensign*, October 2016

[10] 2 Nephi 32:3; Job 23:12

ADDITIONAL STUDY MATERIAL

Most of the following references are referenced throughout this book, but I thought it would be helpful to have them all in one place. The teachings found in them provide the framework for the concepts taught in this book, and are some incredible modern-day scripture about the process of personal revelation.

- "Acquiring Spiritual Knowledge," Elder Richard G. Scott, *Ensign*, November 1993; "To Acquire Spiritual Knowledge," Elder Richard G. Scott, *Ensign*, November 2009
- "Agency or Inspiration — Which?" Elder Bruce R. McConkie, BYU Devotional, February 27, 1973
- "And Upon the Handmaids in Those Days Will I Pour Out My Spirit," Sister Julie B. Beck, *Ensign*, May 2010
- "Change: It's Always a Possibility!" Sister Wendy Watson Nelson, BYU Devotional, April 7, 1998;
- "Continuing Revelation," President Henry B. Eyring, *Ensign*, November 2013
- "Did You Get the Right Message?" President James E. Faust, *Ensign*, May 2004
- "Focus and Priorities," Elder Dallin H. Oaks, *Ensign*, May 2001
- "Gifts of the Spirit for Hard Times," Elder Henry B. Eyring, *Ensign*, June 2007
- "Give Us This Day Our Daily Bread," Elder D. Todd Christofferson, CES Fireside for Young Adults, January 9, 2011, Brigham Young University
- "How to Learn by the Spirit," Elder Richard G. Scott, *Ensign*, September 2014
- "Learning to Recognize Answers to Prayer," Elder Richard G. Scott, *Ensign*, November 1989
- "Little Children," Elder Boyd K. Packer, *Ensign*, November 1986

- "Opening Our Hearts to Revelation," Elder Patrick Kearon, *Ensign,* August 2013
- "Personal Revelation: The Gift, the Test, and the Promise," President Boyd K. Packer, *Ensign*, November 1994
- "Prayer and Promptings," President Boyd K, Packer, *Ensign*, November 2009
- "Revelation for the Church, Revelation for Our Lives," President Russell M. Nelson, *Ensign*, May 2018
- "Revelation in a Changing World," Elder Boyd K. Packer, *Ensign*, November 1989
- "Reverence Invites Revelation," Elder Boyd K. Packer, *Ensign*, November 1991
- "Stand as True Millennials," Elder Russel M. Nelson, *Ensign*, October 2016
- "Take the Holy Spirit as Your Guide," Elder Larry Wilson, *Ensign*, May 2018
- "Teach Them to Understand," President David A. Bednar, Ricks College Campus Education Week Devotional, June 4, 1998
- "The Holy Ghost," Elder Robert D. Hales, *Ensign*, May 2016
- "The Spirit of Revelation," Elder David A. Bednar, *Ensign*, May 2011
- "The Voice of the Lord," Elder Gerald N. Lund, BYU Speeches, Dec. 2, 1997
- "Timing," Elder Dallin H. Oaks, *Ensign*, November 2003
- "Trust in the Lord," Elder Richard G. Scott, *Ensign*, November 1995
- "What Lack I Yet?" Elder Larry Lawrence, *Ensign*, November 2015

ABOUT THE AUTHORS

Stephen Kent Hunsaker has been teaching in Seminaries and Institutes since 1991, with his current assignment as an instructor at the Logan Institute of Religion at Utah State University. He has also taught in the Washington D.C. and central California areas, and wrote curriculum for the Church's online home-study Seminary program.

Some of his other experiences have included teaching marriage and parenting classes, presenting at various family and parenting conferences, serving on Interfaith Religious Forums, presenting at BYU Education Week, and speaking at youth conferences, firesides, and Especially for Youth all over the United States. Stephen graduated with a Bachelor's of Science in Psychology and a Master's Degree in Family and Human Development, both from Utah State. (Go Aggies!)

Michelle Krelo Hunsaker graduated with a Bachelor's of Science in Elementary Education from USU. She was Utah's Young Mother of the Year in 1999. She has been a teacher, sign language interpreter, dance instructor, choreographer, and musical director off and on over the years, but her full-time job through it all has been "mother."

Stephen and Michelle are the parents of ten children, (and a wonderful daughter-in-law and son-in-law), have their first grandson on the way, and live in beautiful Cache Valley, Utah.

You can find this book for sale as well as other information about the concepts in this book at **www.verticallyconnected.com.**